KING ARTHUR: SHADOWS IN THE MIST

Published by Avalonia

BM Avalonia
London
WC1N 3XX
England, UK

www.avaloniabooks.co.uk

King Arthur: Shadows in the Mist
Copyright © August Hunt 2010

ISBN-10: 1-905297-42-4
ISBN-13: 978-1-905297-42-9

Second Edition, November 2010
Originally published in September 2006, as "Shadows in the Mist"
by August Hunt, ISBN 978-1904524380

Design by Satori

Cover Art *"How Mordred was slain by Arthur, and how by him Arthur was hurt to the death"* from *The Romance of King Arthur and his knights of the Round Table,* abridged from *Malory's Morte d'Arthur* by Alfred W.Pollard, Illustrated by Arthur Rackham, 1917.

British Library Cataloguing in Publication Data. A catalogue record for this book is available from the British Library.

ABOUT THE AUTHOR: AUGUST HUNT

August Hunt has a lifelong passion for the Arthurian myths and has been studying them since his youth, which is also when his passion for writing first emerged. His first short stories appeared in his high school newspaper in the 1970's, and since then he has received scholarships and literary prizes for his fictional work, and has written numerous magazine articles, books, novels and screenplays.

He has lectured extensively on the Arthurian myths and related Dark Age topics at colleges and events, and has acted as consultant on television documentaries about King Arthur for the Discovery Channel and National Geographic. His works on the Arthurian mythos and other Dark Age topics are also featured on various award-winning websites.

Drawing on his considerable knowledge of folklore, Celtic myth, onomastics and Dark Age history, August Hunt is providing new and challenging material which illuminates many of the previously shadowy areas of the Arthurian tradition.

August holds a degree in Celtic and Germanic Studies, and is a member of the International Arthurian Society. When he is not engaged in his research and writing, he enjoys hiking and landscaping, with unusual passions such as designing and erecting modern stone circles and monuments which reproduce the solar equinoctial and solstitial alignments of their ancient European counterparts.

His other books include:

The Secrets of Avalon: An Introduction to Arthurian Druidism, 2010, Avalonia

From Within the Mist (anthology), 2004, Double Dragon

Doomstone, 2002, Double Dragon

The Road of the Sun: Travels of the Zodiac King in European and Near Eastern Myth, 1988, Labyrinthos

You can write to the Author:

August Hunt,
c/o Avalonia, BM Avalonia, London, WC1N 3XX, England, UK

Also see: www.secretsofavalon.co.uk

KING ARTHUR

SHADOWS IN THE MIST

**A QUEST FOR THE HISTORICAL KING
ARTHUR IN DARK AGE BRITAIN**

AUGUST HUNT

FOREWORD BY JOHN MATTHEWS

TO MY BROTHER, GALEN
For All of the Adventures

LIST OF IMAGES

TABLE OF CONTENTS

"It is all true, or it ought to be; and more and better besides."

Sir Winston Churchill,
on the legend of King Arthur

Key to *Map of Battle Locations and Significant Places*

1. River Glen (mouth of)
2. Bassington (Bassas River)
3. Devil's Water (near Corbridge)
4. Caledonian Wood (surrounding Eildon Hills)
5. Binchester (Castle Guinnion)
6. York (City of the Legion)
7. River Avon estuary near where it joins the Firth of Forth (Tribruit shore)
8. High Rochester (Breguoin/Bremenium)
9. Catterick (Mount Agned)
10. Buxton (Badon)
11. Castlesteads ('Camlann' Roman fort site)
12. Burgh-By-Sands (Avalon)
13. Stanwix (site of the Uxellodunum fort, Arthur's primary centre)
14. Corbridge Roman fort (Camelot)
15. Hadrian's Wall

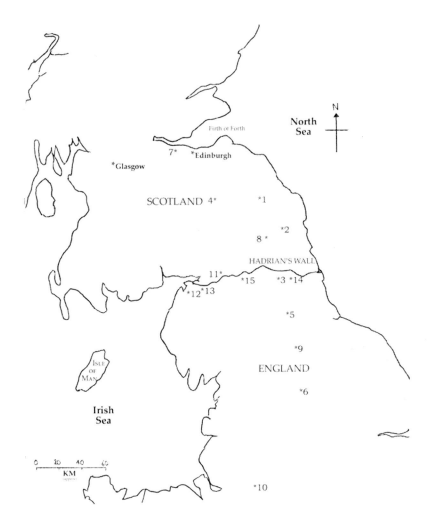

FIGURE 1 - MAP OF BATTLE LOCATIONS & SIGNIFICATION PLACES

For friend and foe were shadows in the mist,

And friend slew friend not knowing whom he slew;

And some had visions out of golden youth,

And some beheld the faces of old ghosts

Look in upon the battle; and in the mist

Was many a noble deed, many a base,

And chance and craft and strength in single fights

And ever and anon with host to host

Shocks, and the splintering spear; the hard mail hewn,

Shield-breakings, and the clash of brands, the crash

Of battleaxes on shattered helms, and shrieks

After the Christ, of those who falling down

Looked up for heaven, and only saw the mist;

And shouts of heathen and the traitor knights,

Oaths, insult, filth, and monstrous blasphemies,

Sweat, writhings, anguish, labouring of the lungs

In that close mist, and cryings for the light,

Moans of the dying, and voices of the dead.

'The Passing of Arthur'
from *Idylls of the King*, Alfred Lord Tennyson

ACKNOWLEDGMENTS

I owe a great debt of gratitude to Dr. Richard Coates of the University of the West of England, Dr. Andrew Breeze of The University of Navarre and Dr. Isaac Graham of the National University of Ireland, Galway, for their acumen in treating of many word problems, tricky and obscure, and to Robert Vermaat, whose critical attention to many of my ideas often served to separate reasonable argument from mere fanciful construction. Finally, I would like to extend my heartfelt appreciation to photographer Ann Bowker, who literally climbed over hill and dale to get the photos that became such an integral part of this book, and to John Matthews, who not only supplied the excellent Foreword, but who offered much sage advice on revision of the manuscript. My heartfelt appreciation also goes out to the following correspondents, whose kindness, patience and dedication helped me put the pieces of the Arthurian puzzle together: Elizabeth O'Brien, UCD Mícheál Ó Cléirigh Institute; Andrew Hawke, National Dictionary of Wales; Peter Wihl, Carmarthenshire place-name expert; Dafydd Hawkins, Powys place-name expert; Kevin Coyle, University of Ottawa; Paul Cavill, The English Place-Name Society; Chris Chandler of English Heritage; Andrew Deathe, Salisbury Museum; Hywel Wyn Owen, University of Wales, Bangor; Richard Coates, University of the West of England; Padraig O Riain, University College, Cork; Sigmund Eisner, University of Arizona, Emeritus; Gareth Bevans, National Library of Wales; Hoyt Greeson, Department of English, Laurentian University; Paul Acker, Saint Louis University; Gregory S. Uchrin, Catholic University of America; Jean-Yves le Moing; Christian Rogel, Director of the Bibliotheque du Finistere, Quimper; Helen McBurnie, Cramlington Parish Secretary; Neil Moffat, Reference and Local Studies Department, Dumfries and Galloway Libraries, Information and Archives, Dumfries and Galloway Council; Peter Drummond, Scottish Place-Name Society; Mark Douglas, Principal Officer for

Heritage and Design, Planning and Economic Development, Scottish Borders Council; Nicola Hunt, Projects Officer of the Borders Forest Trust; Helen Darling, Part-Time Local Studies Librarian, Library Headquarters, St. Mary's Hill, Selkirk; Jennifer Parkson, Map Library, Assistant for the National Library of Scotland; Henry Gough Cooper, Scottish Place-Name Society; Neil Bettridge, Archivist, Derbyshire County Council's Record Office; John Reid, Scottish Place-Name Society; Beatrix Faerber, CELT Project Manager; Ceridwen Lloyd-Morgan, Assistant Archivist, Department of Manuscripts and Records, The National Library of Wales; Brynley F. Roberts, Centre for Advanced Welsh and Celtic Studies, University of Wales; Patrick Sims-Williams, University of Wales; Bruce Jackson, Lancashire County Archivist; Humphrey Welfare, Planning and Development Director, North, English Heritage; Richard Annis, Durham University's Project manager of Archaeological Services; Tim Padley, Keeper of Archaeology, Tullie House Museum and Art Gallery, Carlisle; Georgina Plowright, Curator English Heritage Hadrian's Wall Museums; Stephen White, Carlisle Library; Robert Collins, Newcastle Upon Tyne Museum of Antiquities; Kevan W. White of roman-britain.org; Gill Stroud, Sites and Monument Records Officer, Derbyshire County Council; Ken Smith, Cultural Heritage Manager for the Peak District National Park Authority; John Moreland, Reader at the University of Sheffield, Department of Archaeology' Sue Palmer, Assistant Museums Manager of the Buxton Museum and Art Gallery, Oliver J. Padel, Cambridge University.

LINGUISTIC ABBREVIATIONS USED

AS = Anglo-Saxon
B = British
Br = Breton
Co = Cornish
Lat = Latin
ME = Middle English
MW = Middle Welsh
OE = Old English
OI = Old Irish
ON = Old Norse
OScand = Old Scandinavian
OW = Old Welsh
W = Welsh

CIL = Corpus Inscriptionum Latinarum (a comprehensive collection of Latin inscriptions from across the Roman Empire)
MS = Manuscript
RIB = Roman Inscriptions of Britain

FIGURE 2 - HOW MORDRED WAS SLAIN BY ARTHUR, AND HOW BY HIM ARTHUR
WAS HURT TO THE DEATH BY ARTHUR RACKHAM

FOREWORD

BY JOHN MATTHEWS

The identity, even the existence, of Arthur continues to vex the minds of scholars as keenly as it has done since the Middle Ages. Sir Thomas Malory, in his epic *Le Morte d'Arthur*, speculated on the possible end of the great king, incidentally establishing his legend for all time:

> *"Yet some men say in many parts of England that Arthur is not dead, but had by the will of Our Lord Jesu into another place; and men say that he shall come again, and he shall win the Holy Cross. I will not say it shall be so... but many men say that there is written upon his tomb this verse: Hic Jacet Arthurus, Rex quondam, Rexque Futurus." [Here lies Arthur – the Once and Future King] Le Morte d'Arthur,* Book xxi, ch. vii.

Since that time oceans of ink and forests of paper have been expended in a variety of attempts to identify Arthur; to prove or disprove whether or not he existed, as well as where and when he might have lived and what sort of person he was. Some scholars have set out specifically to show that there was no Arthur; that he is nothing more than a myth, or that if he lived at all he was a minor and unimportant figure in the long history of Britain. Others have put forward claims both believable and bizarre, placing Arthur in Cornwall, in Wales, in Scotland, even in Ireland. Yet no one to date has produced an argument convincing enough to persuade the skeptics, or detailed enough to stand up to the rigours of scholarly examination.

Part of the problem comes from the fact that we have virtually no written evidence from the period when Arthur may have lived. We are not talking about the medieval period described so vividly by Malory, but instead the so-called Dark Ages, now more commonly referred to as the

Early Middle Ages or the Post-Roman period. This was a time of great confusion, when the Celtic tribes, previously held in check by the presence of the legions of Rome, fell back into a familiar pattern of internecine strife and struggle for supremacy. At the same time invaders from across the seas, lumped together under the name of the Saxons, began to raid more deeply into the heartlands of the country, while the wild Picts broke through the ancient line of Hadrian's Wall, leaving a trail of decimated homesteads in their wake. Irish raiders came in from the west.

It is in this period that Arthur entered the stage. Not as a king, but as a charismatic leader and a skillful warrior, whose presence and deeds established him so firmly in the consciousness of the people that he would never be forgotten. It is from this point that the legends of Arthur begin. So many layers have been added to the original history of the time that it has become increasingly difficult to separate fact from fiction, at least with recourse to the few sparse documents remaining to us. The very scarcity of this material forces those who wish to discover the truth about Arthur back into the disciplines of archaeology, place-names and geography. It is to these disciplines in particular that August Hunt has turned in this fascinating new exploration into the mystery of Arthur.

By treating the landscape itself almost like a book, by reading the hints and clues hidden there in the ancient place-names of Celtic Britain, he has uncovered new and convincing evidence that gives a context to the 'Arthurian' period which has in many cases been missing from previous accounts. At the heart of this book lies a reconsideration of twelve great battles fought by Arthur against the Saxons. These are listed in one of the earliest surviving accounts of his deeds, the ninth-century *Historia Brittonum*, supposedly complied by the monk Nennius within three hundred years of Arthur's passing. The locations of these battle-sites have themselves been fought over, quite literally, by a variety of amateurs and experts, with numerous suggestions being put forward.

August Hunt brings a bold new interpretation to Arthur's military sphere, in the process adding his voice to an increasingly large chorus of voices that place the famous war-leader not in the West Country, which has claimed him for many hundreds of years, but in the north of Britain, along the borders between England and Scotland. So much evidence now points to northern locations for places such as Camlan, the site of Arthur's last battle; Avalon, where he is believed to be buried; even to the fabled city of Camelot. Whether or not one believes in the existence of Arthur, or is convinced by August Hunt's arguments, the latter should have the effect of causing some radical rethinking about the reality of Arthur, and just where in the country is the most likely locale for the deeds that made him famous.

August Hunt has indeed found new shadows in the mists of time, and succeeds, in many cases, in dispelling some of the fog that has obscured the truth about Arthur through the centuries. I applaud the publication of this book, which is bound to create some lively discussion and fuel the debate over Arthurian history for some time to come.

John Matthews
Oxford

THE KING WHO ONCE WAS

INTRODUCTION

What little we know of an *'historical'* Arthur is contained in two early medieval works: the *Historia Brittonum*[1] or *History of the Britons*, ascribed to the Welsh monk Nennius, and the anonymous *Annales Cambriae* or *Welsh Annals*. These two sources supply us with the names of thirteen Arthurian battle sites. Twelve of these battles were supposedly fought against the invading Saxons, while one may have involved a conflict with another British chieftain named Medraut, the Mordred of later Arthurian romance.

The first twelve of these battles are all found in the HB immediately after mention of Aesc son of Hengist's rise to the kingship in Kent, an event dated to 488 CE in the *Anglo-Saxon Chronicle*, and just prior to a section dealing with the Saxon kingdom of Bernicia and its king, Ida. Bernicia, coupled with Deira, comprised what became known as Northumbria, i.e. that portion of Britain that extends from the Humber River in the south to the Firth of Forth in the north. Ida began to rule, according to the ASC, circa 547 CE.

The thirteenth battle, that of Camlan, is found only in the AC, where it is dated to 537 CE. Thus the thirteen battles of Arthur are chronologically fixed within the period of 488 to 547 CE or from the latter part of the 5th century to the middle of the 6th. While several alternate chronologies have been proposed for the ASC and certain entries of the AC, for the sake of clarity the traditional dates will be allowed to stand.

The list of Arthurian battle sites, in the order that they occur in the HB and the AC, are as follows:

---

[1] Abbreviated HB (Historia Brittonum), AC (Annales Cambriae) and ASC (Anglo-Saxon Chronicle) in future references.

1) *ostium fluminis quod dicitur* Glein, mouth of the river Glein
2), 3), 4) & 5) *flumen quod dicitur Dubglas, et est in regione Linnuis*, river Dubglas in the Linnuis region
6) *flumen quod vocatur Bassas*, river Bassas
7) *silva Celidonis, id est Cat Coit Celidon*, Celidon Wood, Battle of Celidon Wood
8) *castello Guinnion*, castle of Guinnion
9) *urbe Legionis*, City of the Legion
10) *litore fluminis quod vocatur Tribruit*, river-shore Tribruit
11) *monte qui dicitur Agned*, mount Agned
or
  monte qui nominator Breguoin, mount Breguoin
12) *Badonis (AC), monte Badonis (HB)*, mount Badon (cf. *Badonici montis of Gildas*, who first mentioned Badon in his 6th century work, *De Excidio Brittonum, The Ruin of Britain*)
13) *Camlann* (AC), Camlan

In the HB, Arthur is called a dux bellorum or *'leader of battles'*, and is said to have fought alongside British kings against the pagan barbarians. It is from this bare listing of battle sites that the great body of Arthurian literature – the so-called *'Matter of Britain'* – has grown. The consensus view among Arthurian scholars today is that the subsequent poems, stories, pseudo-histories and romances focusing on Arthur and his court are so heavily fictionalized, so overlaid with mythic, legendary and folkloristic elements, as to be worthless for the study of Arthur as a true Dark Age personage.

There are even those who dispense with the HB and AC Arthurian accounts as well, claiming that there is no way for us to substantiate the genuineness of either. Some scholars go even further in refusing to accept as historically viable in entirety the HB or AC themselves. Indeed, to many the HB is no more than a hodge-podge of historical traditions which in all likelihood has little bearing on the actual events that transpired in Dark Age Britain.

A complication concerns the inability to clearly identify the place-names supplied in the battle list. The tendency has existed for some time to *'make the places fit the theory'*, rather than the opposite. Thus Arthur has been situated just about everywhere in Britain. Artificial geographical patterns have been sought for the battles in order to pinpoint Arthur's power centre and shed dubious light on his origins. Sound philological principles have all too often gone by the wayside when treating of Arthurian place-names. It is precisely the inability to satisfactorily pin down Arthur's battles that has led some scholars to give up the quest and join with those who insist on his non-historicity. For without firm battle site identifications, nothing of the historical Arthur can be known.

To counter the argument that refuses to acknowledge the validity of the battle list, the two Arthurian entries in the AC have frequently been cited. These entries are typical, dry, bare-boned annalistic accounts of battles. Arthur, Medraut and the battle sites of Mt. Badon and Camlan are mentioned in the context of many other proper and place-names, all of which are demonstrably historical in nature. According to this line of reasoning, we need not doubt the veracity of the two entries.

516 an. Bellum Badonis, in quo Arthur portavit crucem Domini nostri Jesu Christi tribus diebus et tribus noctibus in humeros suos et Brittones victores fuerunt.

"The Battle of Badon, in which Arthur carried the cross of our Lord Jesus Christ for three days and three nights on his shoulders and the Britons were the victors."

537 an. Gueith Camlann in quo Arthur et Medraut corruerunt, et mortalitas in Brittannia et Hibernia fuit.

"The Battle of Camlan, in which Arthur and Medraut fell, and there was plague in Britain and Ireland."

Mt. Badon and Camlan are both, however, subject to the same kind of geographical shuffling as the other battle sites. Cases have been made for northern and southern Badons and Camlans. Few have been particularly convincing. Also, what may be legendary accretions similar to those present in the HB's description of Arthur's battle at Castellum Guinnion are to be found in the AC entry on Badon.

> *Octavum fuit bellum in castello Guinnion, in quo Arthur portavit imaginem sanctae Mariae perpetuae virginis super humeros suos, et pagani versi sunt in fugam in illo die, et caedes magna fuit super illos per virtutem Domini nostril Jesu Christi et per virtutem sanctae Mariae virginis benetreis ejus.*

> "The eighth battle was in Castle Guinnion, and in it Arthur carried the image of the holy Mary, the everlasting Virgin, on his [shield], and the heathen were put to flight on that day, and there was a great slaughter of them, through the power of our Lord Jesus Christ and the power of the holy Virgin Mary, his mother."

Such embellishments have convinced many that the Badon entry in the AC should be disqualified as a record of a true Arthurian battle. In this case, it can be plausibly argued that the AC Badon entry has been contaminated by the HB's account of Arthur's battle at Castle Guinnion. This is not to say that Badon itself is denied status as an historical event; only that the placement of Arthur at Gildas's Badon should be interpreted as an instance of hero-making and nothing more.

Gildas himself neglected to include in his work the name of the British commander at Badon:

> *26. ... usque ad annum obsessionis Badonici montis, novissimaeque ferme de furciferis non minimae stragis...*

> "This lasted right up till the year of the siege of Mount Badon, pretty well the last defeat of the villains, and certainly not the least."

Admittedly, in recent years there has been a sort of cautious reaction to the views set forth by proponents of a non-historical Arthur. While respecting the limitations imposed by the nature of the earliest Arthurian sources, limitations that the critical analysis of texts has largely defined, a handful of scholars have made significant headway in dealing with what they believe to be a fundamental over-statement of the problem of Arthur's historicity. These scholars do not object to the actual process of critical analysis, but to some of the conclusions that have been drawn from the results of such analysis. The said conclusions, when treated of logically, can be revealed as arbitrarily formed and thus are reflections of expert opinion or even prejudice or bias, and not objective fact.

The 'Arthur Problem', put in the simplest terms, is this: is there sufficient reason for seeing the Arthur of the HB and AC as a plausible historical entity? Those who choose to see Arthur as a non-historical personage may strenuously object to this question. They would doubtless prefer that the problem be stated differently, e.g. is there sufficient evidence for seeing the Arthur of the sources as a historical entity?

Unfortunately, demanding evidence of the kind that would satisfy the proponents of the non-historical view automatically removes Arthur from the realm of historical study. Happening upon complimentary textual evidence from a source or sources deemed authentic and dependable seems a remote possibility. Archaeology, despite the ever-increasing light it sheds on Britain's Dark Age past, has so far failed to yield anything substantive on Arthur. By refusing to allow for the possibility that Arthur may conceivably be historical, scholars engage in a sort of self-fulfilling prophecy, the fulfillment of which can only be that Arthur will continue to be found ineligible for historical status. Along with maintaining such perpetual ineligibility is a steadfast refusal on the part of scholars to allow interested parties to engage in research that might be deemed related even tangentially to Arthur as a possible historical phenomenon.

It may ultimately prove true that the only value in further analysis of Arthur's battle sites might be an elucidation of the 9th century's perspective on and attitude towards a reputed 5th-6th century British war-leader. Granted, there is some indication that the battle list as found in the HB is not an artificial construction undertaken by the monk Nennius, but instead preserves the content, rather than strictly the form, of a much earlier heroic poem originally composed in Arthur's honor. If this widely held view is correct, then the battle list may reflect something other than a late traditional portrait of Arthur. It may be much more of a contemporary record of campaigns than the 9th century source in which it is embedded might otherwise suggest.

Still, if findings that arise from additional probing into the probable locations of Arthurian battle sites accomplish nothing other than to bring more into focus how the 9th century Britons interpreted their own remote past, then we will still have greatly advanced our knowledge of the period.

The burden of proof is just as much on the shoulders of those who dismiss Arthur as non-historical as it is on those who conditionally accept him as historical. Such an acknowledgment forces us to accept the possibility that Arthur existed without having to entertain the probability. If it can be demonstrated, based upon our knowledge of his battles, that an Arthur in the time period under consideration is a plausible phenomenon, then we can open a doorway into new areas of intellectual endeavor whose express purpose is to provide the impetus for the eventual discovery of evidence needed to historicize this British war-leader.

If there were to be an implied philosophy underlying this book, it would be that scholars of Arthuriana or Dark Age Britain ought not to view with disdain objective exploration of the potential historicity of Arthur. For as it may well turn out, the sources we do possess for the military career of this Dark Age figure may prove to have validity after all. While the means of providing such validity are currently not available to us, to state as fact that Arthur is not a historical entity or that we are not justified in seeing him as being even plausibly historical, is to risk making one of the biggest blunders imaginable in the annals of academic investigation.

It is the business of Arthurian and Dark Age scholars to consider possibilities. By possibilities is not meant, of course, wild theories that have no hope of ever being substantiated. Instead, possibilities in this context can best be defined as plausible historic scenarios that, while they may not be testable at the moment, may prove to be so in the future. Such scenarios must, needless to say, fit into the general, though wonderfully complex and interdependent tapestry created for us by universally accepted disciplines of study.

As more and more data comes in from these disciplines, and the resulting picture of the past is altered or refined accordingly, those scenarios that fail to conform in a manner deemed appropriate can be dispensed with. Eventually, with the aid of increasingly sophisticated scientific tools, our knowledge of Dark Age British history will be much greater than it is now. Most plausible scenarios will have been discarded. An historical Arthur might well be one of these casualties. Only a few scenarios – perhaps, if we are extraordinarily fortunate, just one – will remain solvent.

But until then, summarily deleting Arthur from the pages of our history books is not an ethical or reasonable solution to the 'Arthur Problem'. It would be wiser and less shortsighted to include him, albeit with the necessary caveats. Any further evidence that supported Arthur's historicity could thus be uncovered earlier, rather than later.

The present book, therefore, operates under the premise that precisely because Arthur may be historical, it would be intellectually prudent to apply more effort to the study of the only textual evidence we do have regarding this Dark Age British war-leader, i.e. the battles listed in the HB and AC. On the other hand, to ignore the battles themselves as possible historical events would be to intentionally turn a blind eye to evidence that has not yet been thoroughly evaluated. Potentially, a comprehensive examination of the battle sites, if undertaken with no agenda, nationalistic or otherwise, might harvest some new information on Arthur. And any new information, whether it ends up contributing arguments for or against a historical personage, is the proper goal of true scholarship.

The method employed by the author will be to utilize sound philological and geographical principles in the context of the Arthurian battles in order to arrive at several new site identifications. Included in this analysis, by necessity, will be a brief consideration of those past and present identifications deemed to be of a more respectable nature. But first will come some speculation regarding the period just before Arthur, with special emphasis on the figures of Ambrosius, Cunedda and Vortigern. Arthur's origins will then be explored, utilizing the earliest versions of ancient Welsh genealogies, as well as the etymology of the name Arthur and its historical attestations in both Roman and Dark Age Britain. The remainder of the book will explore the Dark Age British kingdoms in the North and the power centres and grave of Arthur. These various investigations will produce a theoretical reconstruction of the life and death of *'King Arthur'*.

The reader should understand that many proper and place-name authorities have been consulted in the preparation of this book, either via personal correspondence or through their published works or both, and I have listed these generous and often patient contributors on my Acknowledgments page and in the Bibliography. Any conclusions I have drawn by relying on scholarly elucidation are solely my own and do not in any way reflect the opinions of the scholars themselves.

CHAPTER 1

BEFORE ARTHUR: AMBROSIUS, CUNEDDA AND VORTIGERN

1) AMBROSIUS

Aurelius Ambrosius, said to be a Roman, is the most famous figure in Dark Age British history prior to Arthur. Why? Because he is credited with having united the Britons in a successful defense of the country against the Saxons, who from Vortigern's time had, according to the traditional account, pillaged and conquered at will.

Ambrosius is important also because it has been fashionable to identify him with Arthur. As we shall see, such an identification is impossible.

To begin, Ambrosius was not a contemporary of Arthur. He was not, in fact, even a contemporary of Vortigern, who preceded Arthur by a century. And this is true despite the HB account, which brings Vortigern and Ambrosius (as the Welsh Emrys) together for a fabulous story that takes place at Dinas Emrys in northwestern Wales (see below).

There are three major problems with accepting Ambrosius as a contemporary of Vortigern. First, he cannot have been a Roman and been in Britain during or after Vortigern's rule. The withdrawal of the Romans is firmly dated at c. 409 CE. Vortigern's ruling dates, depending on the sources consulted, are anywhere from twenty to forty years after the Roman withdrawal. If he were a Roman during or after Vortigern, then he came from the Continent and was not a native Briton. The argument could be made that *'Romanized'* Britons continued to preserve the Roman way of life in southern England for a half century after the withdrawal of the troops. In this sense, a chieftain like Ambrosius might still consider himself to be *'Roman'*.

However, the HB tells us that Ambrosius fought a battle against a certain Vitalinus at a Guoloph or Wallop, thought to be the Hampshire Wallop. This Vitalinus is listed in the HB as the grandfather of Vortigern. This means that Ambrosius has wrongly been placed in the time of Vortigern. He actually belongs to the time of Vitalinus, who was probably of the 4th century.

The father of the famous 4th century St. Ambrose bore the name Aurelius Ambrosius. This man was, furthermore, the prefect or governor of Gaul (Gallia). Britain, Spain and Gaul were in the Gallic prefecture. So, we have here a historical figure named Aurelius Ambrosius who not only was a true *'Roman'*, but who could have had something to do with military operations carried out in Britain in the 4th century.

There is good reason to believe that St. Ambrose himself bore the name Aurelius. Jones' *Prosopography of the Later Roman Empire* gives no second name for the bishop of Milan and neither does Paulinus of Milan's *Vita*. Ambrose may have belonged to the gens Aurelia, as we know that he was related to Symmachus [Quintus Aurelius Symmachus]; an inscription refers to him as *Aurelius Ambrosius*. It is true that there is a debate over the Ambrose referred to in the inscription. Those who think it is Ambrose junior [St. Ambrose] point out that a dedication to St. Nazarius is involved. The point may be moot: if Ambrose senior belonged to the gens Aurelia, so did the son, and vice versa.

One other factor strongly indicates that there is no good historical reason for accepting a 5th century Aurelius Ambrosius in Britain. Vortigern's only interaction with Ambrosius, or Emrys Guletic (*'Prince Ambrosius'*) as he is called in Welsh tradition, is in the Dinas Emrys folktale already alluded to above.

Other than Dinas Emrys, there appears to be no site in Britain which can be shown to contain the personal name Ambrosius. Still, this hero may even have been placed at Guoloph/Wallop because of the proximity of this stream to

Amesbury. As Geoffrey of Monmouth did much later, Ambrosius's name was fancifully associated with Amesbury. The town name does not, in fact, seem to contain the personal name Ambrosius. Its etymology is instead as follows:

Ambresbyrig, from a c.880 CE charter, then various spellings to Amblesberie in *Domesday*. Almost certainly a personal name *Ambre* or *Aembre* cognate with the Old German *Ambri*, hence Ambre's burgh, cf. Ombersley. All the early forms for Amesbury have the medial -b-, but no form has any extension that would justify derivation from Ambrosius.

Ambrosius as a Latin adjective means *"the Divine or Immortal One"*. As such, it was at some point taken to be a title for the Welsh god Lleu. Welsh tradition made Lleu the ancient ruler of Gwynedd, and this is the rank granted to Emrys or Ambrosius in the HB. Hence Dinas Emrys in northwestern Wales, the *'[Hill-] fort of the Divine or Immortal One'*, is actually the Fort of Lleu.

The Welsh also appear to have identified the youthful god Mabon with Lleu. That this is so is demonstrated by the placement of the two gods in death at the same place. According to the *Mabinogion* tale *Math Son of Mathonwy*, Lleu is found as the death-eagle in the oak tree at Nantlle (Nant Lleu) in Snowdonia not far from Dinas Emrys. And one of the *Stanzas of the Graves* reads:

> *"The grave on Nantlle's height,*
>
> *No one knows its attributes –*
>
> *Mabon son of Modron the Swift."*

In Chapter 6, we will discuss Emrys's Campus Elleti, supposedly a site in southern Wales, in the context of Camelot. There it will be shown that Campus Elleti is a relocation of a northern Arthurian ruling centre.

Geoffrey of Monmouth proceeded to further confuse the story of Ambrosius, a Roman governor of Gaul mistakenly identified with a Welsh god, by identifying both with the Northern Myrddin or Merlin. Hence we find Merlin or *'Merlin Ambrosius'* in the Dinas Emrys story of Emrys/Lleu/Mabon.

In addition, Merlin is placed at the springs of Galabes, Geoffrey's attempt at the Guoloph of the hero Ambrosius.

In conclusion, we can only say that there is no good reason for supposing that Vortigern and Ambrosius were contemporaries. Instead, the Ambrosius mentioned by Gildas as having military success in Britian must have been the 4th century Gallic governor of that name. This being the case, Ambrosius could not possibly have been the victor at the battle of Mount Badon, which is dated 516 CE. And, by extension, Ambrosius was not Arthur.

2) CUNEDDA

The great Cunedda is said to have come down (or been brought down) from Manau Gododdin, a region around the head of the Firth of Forth, to Gwynedd. This chieftain and his sons then, according to the account found in the HB, proceeded to repulse Irish invaders. Unfortunately, this tradition is largely mistaken. To prove that this is so, we need to begin by looking at the famous Wroxeter Stone, found at the Viroconium Roman fort in what had been the ancient kingdom of the Cornovii, but which was the kingdom of Powys in the Dark Ages.

The Wroxeter Stone is a memorial to a chieftain named Cunorix son of Maquicoline. This stone has been dated c. 460-75 CE. Maquicoline is a composite name meaning Son [Maqui-] of Coline. The resemblance here of Cunorix and Coline to the ASC's Cynric and his son Ceawlin is obvious. Some scholars would doubtless say this is coincidence, and that the discrepancy in dates for Cynric and Ceawlin and Cunorix and (Maqui)coline are too great to allow for an identification. I would say that an argument based on the very uncertain ASC dates is hazardous at best and that if there is indeed a relationship between the pairs Ceawlin-Cynric and Coline-Cunorix, then the date of the memorial stone must be favored over that of the document.

There is also the problem of Cynric being the father of Ceawlin in the Anglo-Saxon tradition, while on the Wroxeter Stone it is (Maqui)coline who is the father of Cunorix. But such a confusion could easily have occurred simply by reading part of a genealogy list backwards.

While Ceawlin's father Cynric, the son of Cerdic of Wessex in most pedigrees, is capable of being derived quite well from Anglo-Saxon, the name could also be construed as an Anglicized form of the attested Celtic name Cunorix, Hound-king, the latter Welsh Cynyr.

Cerdic (= Ceredig) is not the only Celtic name in the early Wessex pedigree. Scholars have suggested that Ceawlin could be Brittonic.

Cunorix son of Maquicoline, based on an analysis of his name and the lettering employed on the inscription itself, is believed to have been Irish. It should not surprise us, then, to find Cunedda of Manau Gododdin, the reputed founder of Gwynedd, was himself actually Irish. There was an early St. Cuindid (d. c. 497 CE) son of Cathbad, who founded a monastery at Lusk, ancient Lusca. In the year entry 498 CE of the *Ulster Annals*, his name is spelled Chuinnedha. In Tigernach 496 CE, the name is in the form Cuindedha.

The Irish sources also have the following additional information concerning St. Cuindid:

Mac Cuilind - Cunnid proprium nomen - m. Cathmoga m. Cathbath m Cattain m Fergossa m. Findchada m Feic m. Findchain m Imchada Ulaig m. Condlai m Taide m. Cein m Ailella Olum.

> *U496.2 Quies M. Cuilinn episcopi Luscan. (Repose of Mac Cuilinn, bishop of Lusca).*
>
> *D.viii. idus Septembris.*
>
> *993] Luscai la Macc Cuilinn*
>
> *994] caín decheng ad-rannai,*
>
> *995] féil Scéthe sund linni,*
>
> *996] Coluimb Roiss gil Glandai.*

trans: 'With Macc cuilinn of Luscae thou apportionest (?) a fair couple: the feast of Sciath here we have, (and that) of Columb of bright Ross Glandae'

The (later-dated) notes to this entry read: *'Lusk, i.e. in Fingall, i.e. a house that was built of weeds (lusrad) was there formerly, and hence the place is named Lusca ....Macc cuilinn, i.e. Luachan mac cuilinn, ut alii putant. Cuinnid was his name at first, Cathmog his father's name'.*

Significantly, Lusk or Lusca is a very short distance from the huge promontory fort at Drumanagh, the Bruidhne Forgall Manach of the ancient Irish tales. Drumanagh is the hill of the Manapii and, as such, represents the Manapia in Manapii territory found on the map of Ptolemy. Manapii or Manapia could easily have been mistaken or substituted for for the Manau in Gododdin.

Aeternus, Cunedda's father, is none other than Aithirne of Dun and Ben Etair just south of Lusca. Paternus Pesrudd (*'Red-Cloak'*), Cunedda's grandfather, is probably not derived from Mac Badairn of Es Ruad (*'Red Waterfall'*), since Es Ruad is in northwest Ireland (Ballyshannon in Co. Donegal). I think Paternus, from the L. word for *'father'*, is Da Derga, the Red God; Da, god, being interpreted as W. *tad* (cf. L. *tata*, *'father'*). The Da Derga's hostel was just a little south of the Liffey. Cunedda's great-great-grandfather is said to be one Tegid (Tacitus), while his great-great-great grandfather is called Cein. These two chieftains are clearly Taig/Tadhg and his father Cian. Cian was the founder of the Irish tribe the Ciannachta, who ruled Mag Breg, a region situated between the Liffey and either Duleek or Drumiskin (depending on the authority consulted). The Lusca and Manapia of Chuinnedha are located in Mag Breg.

According to the genealogy edited in *Corpus Genealogiarum Sanctorum Hiberniae*, the name of Mac Cuilind's father was Cathmug. He belonged to the descendants of Tadc mac Cian, otherwise called the Cianachta. There was a concentration of the saints of this family in the Dublin/Louth/ Meath area, corresponding roughly to the teritory of the Cianachta Breg.

It is surely not a coincidence that according to the *Irish Annals* Chuinnedha's other name was Mac Cuilinn. Obviously, Mac Cuilinn and the Maqui-Coline of the Wroxeter Stone are the same name and hence the same person. Gwynedd was thus founded by Chuinnedha alias Mac Cuilinn of the Manapii in Ireland, not by a chieftain of Manau Gododdin in Britain.

The Irish origin of Cunedda should not be a surprise to us, as there is the well-documented case of the Welsh genealogy of the royal house of Dyfed, which was altered to hide the fact that Dyfed was founded by the Irish Deisi. We know this because we have the corresponding Irish genealogy from a saga which tells of the expulsion of the Deisi from Ireland and their settlement in Dyfed. As is true of Cunedda's pedigree, in the Welsh Dyfed pedigree we find Roman names substituted for Irish names. There were other Irish-founded kingdoms in Wales as well, e.g. Brycheiniog.

What exactly the relationship was that existed between Cunedda and the British kingdom of Powys on the one hand, and Cunedda/Ceawlin of the Gewissei (the *'Sure or Reliable Ones'*) and the Saxons of southern England on the other, is something that can only be surmised once we plug Vortigern into the equation. While it is true that Bede called Ceawlin a Bretwalda, i.e. a preeminent ruler of Britain, we are not justified in equating him with Vortigern.

3) VORTIGERN

The name Vortigern or Gwrtheyrn, as found in the HB of Nennius, was once held to be a ruling title. It was thought to be represented by Gildas' Latin pun *'superbus tyrannus'* or *'Proud Tyrant'*. However, we now know that Vortigern was a proper name and not a title. It is found recorded not only in several localities in Wales, but in Ireland as well.

Aside from the British Vortigern, whose name means *'Over-lord'*, we have records for the following Dark Age Irish Vortigerns or *'Fortcherns'*:

1) Fortchern, the smith of St. Patrick (*Annals of the Four Masters* Year Entry 448); as this Fortchern is paired with another smith, Laebhan, i.e. St. Lomman (?), this Fortchern may be:

2) Foirtchern son of Fedelmid, who was for a short time bishop of St. Lomman's Trim. Fortchern of Trim, who was of mixed Irish and British blood, is said to have later retired to Killoughterane/Cill Fortchern in the parish of Muinebeag, Co. Carlow. However, we are told in the ancient Irish sources that Fortchern the smith is the same as Foirtchern of Rath Seimhne (see below). It may not be a coincidence that there is a Gobbin's Cliff, the Cliffs of the divine smith Goban Saor, in Seimhne/Island Magee.

3) Vortigern of Ballyhank, East Muskerry, Co. Cork (inscribed stone).

4) Vortigern of Knockboy in Decies Without Drum, Co. Waterford (inscribed stone dated c. 700-900 CE).

5) Foirtchern of Monte Cainle (probably the Hill of Conlig/Coinleac in north Co. Down), a contemporary of St. Columba.

6) Foirtchern of Rath Seimhne (Island Magee, south Co. Antrim).

7) Fortchern, brother of Cathchern (a name cognate with British Cattigern, a supposed son of Vortigern in the HB narrative), son of Tigernach of the Meic Carthind of the Lough Foyle region.

8) Fortcheirn son of Mael Rubae of the Ui Dicholla of the Dessi

9) Fortchern son of Iarlaith of the Ui Brigte of the Dessi

10) Fortchern son of Tigernach of the Ui Brigte of the Dessi

11) Clan Foirtchern in the Breadach genealogy on Inishowen, near the Lough Foyle Meic Carthind

These examples, some 'in stone', should be sufficient to dispel the notion that Vortigern is merely a title. Instead, Vortigern is a genuine Brythonic personal name.

In Wales, Radnorshire or Maesyfed (the 'field of Hyfaidd') was once known as Gwrtheyrnion, i.e. the kingdom of Gwrtheyrn. Gwrtheyrnion, roughly between the Wye and Ithon rivers, was a relatively small kingdom in southwestern Powys. Other places in Wales where Vortigern's name is preserved are Nant Gwrtheyrn in Lleyn, close to Gwyniasa (and surrounding Gwynus placenames), and a Craig Gwrtheyrn on the Teifi.

These three places are mentioned in Nennius's narrative, but only Gwrtheyrnion carries weight. The Lleyn and Teifi sites may represent the presence in these places of other Vortigerns, but in all likelihood it is merely the proximity to them of St. Garmon place-names that accounts for the *'Overlord's'* association with them. In Nennius's story of Vortigern, the poor chieftain is literally hounded all over Wales by the saint. Thus wherever there was a known St. Garmon site, Vortigern was placed there. In my opinion, Vortigern was probably not in Lleyn, nor was he on the Teifi (despite the presence at nearby Nevern of a Vitalinus Stone; see below). He belonged instead to Gwrtheyrnion, which was merely one of several Welsh Dark Age sub-kingdoms.

Vortigern of Wales, who is said to have been the son of Guitaul (= Roman Vitalis) son of Guitolin (= Roman Vitalinus, a name found on a stone at Nevern dated by Charles Thomas between 466 and 533 CE – too late for Vortigern's grandfather) son of Gloiu (Gloyw, the eponym of Welsh Caerloyw, modern Gloucester), is actually the British-Irish Fortchern son of Fedelmid son of Laeghaire. This Fortchern son of Fedelmid was of the right time to be the Vortigern of Nennius. Both Guitaul and Guitolin are substituted for the name Fedel-mid.

It was Robert Vermaat who first called my attention to the details surrounding this particular Fortchern. To quote extensively from his Vortigern Studies website article, *'Scotnoe & Foirtgirn, the Irish Branch'*:

> *"Foirtchern was the son of Fedelmid, son of Loguire, who was High King of Ireland throughout the period of the mission of St. Patrick (whose dates may be 428-462). Foirtchern's mother was a daughter of the King of the Britons. The story goes that when St. Patrick's nephew Lomman visited Trim (in Ireland), the boy Foirtchernn took him home to Fedelmid and his mother, who both spoke British and were delighted to see a visitor from his mother's country. They made Lomman stay, who then subsequently converted the whole family. The mother might have been a Christian in the*

first place, for she 'welcomed' the saint. Maybe the fact that Lomman was a Christian made him more welcome than his being from Britain. Fedelmid may have embraced Christianity because the saint had just come from Tara Hill, where St. Patrick had defeated the druids of Fedelmid's father the High King Loguire.

Foirtchern's date may be confirmed by the Annala Rioghachta Eirann:

Annals of the Four Masters, M432.0 – 4

The Age of Christ, 432. The fourth year of Laeghaire. Patrick came to Ireland this year, and proceeded to baptize and bless the Irish, men, women, sons, and daughters, except a few who did not consent to receive faith or baptism from him, as his Life relates. Ath Truim was founded by Patrick, it having been granted by Fedhlim, son of Laeghaire, son of Niall, to God and to him, Loman, and Fortchern.

These annals, though dating to 1616 in their youngest version, date back at least to 1172.

In any case, Fedelmid enthrusted Foirtchirnn to Lomman and founded the church of Trim, making St Patrick, Lomman and Foirtchirnn his heirs. But Foirtchernn was obdurate and did not want to accept his heritage, after which Lomman had to threaten him with taking away the blessing of the church, which is tantamount to incurring its curse. After Lomman's death, though, Foirtchirnn gave away his church within three days. This may be apocryphal, for Foirtchirnn was listed afterwards as the first episcopus (abbot) after Fedelmid and Lomman. He might have given it up later though, for he is also listed as a plebilis, a lay successor."

Now, the question on my mind, after reading this account, was *"Who succeeded Lomman at Trim?"* The answer is in the *Patrician Texts* in the *Book of Armagh*:

He [Foirtchernn] held the abbacy for three days after his master's death until he came to Ath Truim, and then immediately handed his church over to the foreigner Cathlaid [Cathlaido perigrino].

I immediately recognized this *'Cathlaid the Foreigner'* as a doublet for Catel Durnluc, the traditional founder of Powys, the kingdom that succeeded that of the Roman-period Cornovii.

Fortchern son of Fedelmid's mixed ancestry allows for the possibility that he possessed or inherited lands on both sides of the Irish Sea. We know that there were several Irish-founded kingdoms in Wales at the time: the Deissi established a ruling dynasty in Dyfed, Brycheiniog was of Irish foundation, and Cunedda of Manau Gododdin, founder of Gwynedd, was actually Chuinnedha/MacCuilind of Drum Managh in Ireland. Cunedda and his sons are said to have chased the Irish out of Anglesey, Dyfed, Gower and Kidwelly, and there is the possibility that Dinevor in Ystrad Tywi was named for an Efwr Llwydon, i.e. of the Irish Leithan. The Irish mercenary Cunorix son of Maquicoline/Cunedda was buried in the heart of Powys at Viroconium. There is no difficulty, then, in accepting a Gwrtheyrnion as a sub-kingdom named after Fortchern son of Fedelmid.

The only objection to a Gwrtherynion ruled by a chieftain of mixed British-Irish ancestry would be that such a king, with such a small sub-kingdom, could not possibly be the *'superbus tyrannus'* of Gildas. But I offer this argument to account for how such a confusion could have taken place: any chieftain possessing a name such Vor-tigern, *'the over-/super-/great- lord'* could easily have been misinterpreted as an over-king similar to the ardrigh or *'high-king'* of Ireland. If I am right and Fortchern son of Fedelmid son of Laeghaire the high king is the British Vortigern of Gwrtheyrnion, then this kind of royal descent from an ardrigh could also have contributed to Gildas's misinterpretation of Vortigern's status in Britain.

In summary, then, what may have happened is this: a chieftain named Vortigern (or Fortchern), who was of mixed Irish-British ancestry, and whose grandfather was the ardrigh of Ireland, had established a small sub-kingdom in southwestern Powys in the 5th century. Gildas, attracted to the name because it seemed to denote a sort of British high king, laid the blame for the Saxon *'invitation'* in this presumed high king's lap. Further vilification continued after this identification of Vortigern as the offending monarch was made, until by the 9th century we have a fully developed story of Vortigern in the HB of Nennius.

Alternately, given that the Eliseg Pillar in what was the kingdom of Powys traces the descent of the Powys dynasty from Vortigern, and Catel Durnluc is in the various genealogies confused with Vortigern or made his near-descendent, it is possible that Fortchern son of Fedelmid, at least partly through his wife's British blood, had managed to lay claim to the throne of Powys itself. His sub-kingdom of Gwrtheyrnion was, after all, part of Powys.

What can be said, with a fair degree of certainty, is that Fortchern son of Fedelmid and the Irish Cunedda were contemporaries. Also, the son of Cunedda was buried in honor at the capital of Powys, Viroconium. Cunedda, his sons and their 'teulu' or war-band composed what the Saxons of southern England came to call the Gewessei, the Sure or Reliable Ones. This teulu fought alongside Saxons against other British in the area. We can assume that as had been the case with Roman federates, Cunedda and his followers were given lands in Gwynedd in return for rendering military service to the old Cornovii kingdom. Even if these lands had been granted in a de facto manner, a peaceful and supportive relationship could be sustained with Powys by the adoption of federate status. Doubtless this process had its origin in the Roman period.

A NOTE ON THE GRAVE OF VORTIGERN

Robert Vermaat has elsewhere written about the *Stanzas of the Graves* which places Gwrtheyrn Gwrtheneu's *'doubtful'* grave at an unlocated Ystyuacheu. To date, all efforts to locate this grave have failed. What follows is an attempt to both find this elusive burial site and to explore its significance in the broader context of just who Vortigern might have been.

The placename Ystyuacheu should be rendered in a more modern fashion as something like Styfacheu/

Stafacheu/Stofacheu. Unfortunately, such a form is also not locatable. It is true, however, that MS. copyists frequently confused the letters u and n. This being so, I propose that perhaps the first -u- of Ystyuacheu might, in fact, have originally been an –n-. This would yield a Stynacheu/Stanacheu/Stonacheu.

In all of Wales, I found only one such Stynacheu/Stanacheu/Stonacheu site which made sense both etymologically and in terms of what we know of Vortigern. This is Stanage on the Teme River in Radnorshire. Stanage is from either OE *stan* + *ecg*, *'stone edge'*, or the ME *stan* + *egge*, with the same meaning.

The difference in the ending of Stanage and a hypothetical Stanageu/Stanagau may be accounted for in the same manner as the process by which the Cymracized English placename Stange became Stangau. These are the forms for Stange/Stangau:

- STANGAU at SN761261 on map sheet SN72 900ft Parish of Llandeusant. 1948 OS 1:25000 First series.
- STANGE 1840 OS 1" first edition (David & Charles reprint).
- STANGAU 1891 OS6" First edition.
- SLANGE 1805-12 OS2" Original Drawing Map.
- RHIW alias STANGE 1808 Blaen Sawdde Estate Map. West Glamorgan Archives, Swansea.

As it turns out, Stange is a dialectal variant of stangau. The writers of some documents quite commonly *'corrected'* the local pronunciation by inserting the standard form.

Stanage has a Welsh equivalent *'y Fron-faen'* (modern spelling, *'the stone breast/steep hillside'*). The English and Welsh versions seem to have existed side-by-side among the relative speech-communities for centuries, but the Welsh version seems to have disappeared around the end of the 16th century, as the Welsh language became extinct in the area.

At Stanage there is an early medieval motte, a medieval mound and bailey castle and medieval Stanage Castle. In my opinion, the motte was thought to represent the *'castle'* in which Vortigern burned to death on the Teifi (according to Nennius). The question then becomes; *'Which tradition is correct'* - that which places Vortigern on the Teifi or that which places him on the Teme?

To begin with, the similarity in the two river names could easily have led to confusion. The oldest forms of the Teme are of the type _Temede_ (which appears in Welsh as _Tefaidd_ (though the name now appears to be lost), while the earliest spellings for _Teifi_ are _Te(i)bi_, with an earlier form in Ptolemy (2nd century CE) _Touegobios_ or _Touerobios_. Teifi and Teme are etymologically related; cf. Thames, in Welsh Tafwys. In terms of etymology, Teme and Teifi are linked because -f- is the result of lenition of earlier Welsh/British -m-.

The truly interesting thing about the Teme site is that it is, as already mentioned, located in Radnorshire. That portion of Radnorshire between the Wye and the Ithon rivers, which lies west of Stanage, was once known as the cantref of Gwrtheyrnion, i.e. the land of Vortigern. Stanage lies in Maelienydd cantref, which bordered on Gwrtheyrnion.

It would seem, therefore, that the original story had Vortigern dying on the Teme near Gwrtheyrnion. This site was transplanted to the Teifi to take advantage of the St. Garmon place-name found there. Geoffrey of Monmouth later moved the site once again, situating it at Ganarew near his home town.

The *'doubtful'* quality assigned to Vortigern's grave at Stange is appropriate, as this king was almost certainly buried at Viroconium.

CHAPTER 2

ARTHUR'S ANCESTRY: RESTORING A GENEALOGY

To find where Arthur ruled, we need to find where his father Uther Pendragon came from. This is not as easy a task as one might think, as Geoffrey of Monmouth and the Welsh genealogists have conspired, through ignorance or a spirit of literary invention or both, to obfuscate Uther's origin.

Despite the fictions which accumulated around Uther, Welsh tradition has sufficient references to Arthur's father that are pre-Galfridian (*'before Geoffrey of Monmouth'*) to prompt us to look for a genuine historical figure.

There are those who would follow the genealogy offered for Uther found in Geoffrey of Monmouth. In that source, Uther was the son of Constantine III, the western emperor who was proclaimed in 407 CE by British troops. Uther's brothers are said to be Constans and Aurelius Ambrosius. As it so happens, Constantine III did have a son Constans, but Aurelius Ambrosius is an anachronism, for that personage was the 4th century prefect of Gaul, father of the much more famous St. Ambrose (see Chapter 1 above).

The reason for the anachronism is simple: the 5th century Constantine III took his name – Flavius Claudius Constantinus – from the 4th century Constantine I the Great. The latter Constantine also had a son named Constans (337-350 CE) with brothers named Constantius II (337-361 CE) and Constantine II (337-340 CE).

The 5th century Constantine III had a younger son named Julian. But both Julian and Constans were killed on the Continent, the first at Arles in 411 and the latter at

Vienne. Although there is some reason to believe that Constans and Julian may originally have borne British names, for chronological reasons alone, neither of these two sons of Constantine III could have been Uther Pendragon.

So if Constantine III was not the father of Uther, and neither Constans nor Ambrosius were the brothers of Uther, how do we possibly find out what kingdom Uther ruled in Britain?

The Welsh genealogy for Arthur follows Geoffrey in the main, making Arthur son of Uther son of Constantine the Blessed (W. *Fendigaid*) or *'of Cornwall'* (W. *Cernyw, Corneu*) son of Cynfor son of Tudwal son of Gwrfawr son of Gadeon son of Eudaf. The sole purpose of this Welsh genealogy, it would appear, was to provide Constantine father of Uther with a Breton origin. This may have been done (although see below) in order to accommodate Geoffrey's claim that Constantine came from Brittany.

This genealogy is patently false. Cynfor the supposed grandfather of Uther is the Cynfor/Cunomorus or Chonomor, Prince of Domnonee in Brittany and probably of Dumnonia in southwestern Britain, who died c. 560 CE. The Drustanus son of Cunomorus stone at Castle Dore in Cornwall has been dated 533-599 CE. Drustanus in the Welsh tradition was Trystan son of Tallwch, an identification with the Pictish king Drostan mac Tallorg. Cynfor /Cunomorus was thus the predecessor of the Constantine who was among the contemporary rulers denounced by the sixth century Gildas. Thus Cynfor cannot possibly have been the grandfather of a fifth century Uther.

If we are willing to free Uther from the artificial pedigree imposed upon him by Geoffrey of Monmouth and the Welsh, a pedigree which has Uther's father Constantine come from Brittany of the 6th century, an excellent solution to the problem of Uther's ancestry may reveal itself to us. In the process, we will be able – for the first time – to adequately explain why the various Arthurs of the late 6th-7th centuries all hail (see below) from Irish-British royal families.

The answer to the riddle of Uther's true origin lies in the identification of Cynfor/Cunomorus with the fabled King

Mark. And this identification, in turn, provides a solution to the mystery of the Mote of Mark in Dumfries. The Mote of Mark fort is not many miles east of a Trusty's Hill fort, i.e. Drustan's/Tristan's Hill, near Gatehouse of Fleet. Beroul's Tristan associates its hero with both Galloway and Dumfries. How can we account for Tristan's and Mark's presence in the far North?

FIGURE 3 - THE MOTE OF MARK

No one has adequetely explained the presence of the names Mark and Drustan in southwestern Lowland Scotland.

The pedigree of the Welsh Mark, or rather March, runs as follows:

- March son of Meirchion son of Custennin son of Kynfarch (sic) son of Tudwal, etc.
- To this we may compare Arthur's pedigree:
  Arthur son of Uther son of Custennin son of Cynfor son of Tudwal, etc.

We notice two things immediately: 1) Cynfarch has been wrongly substituted for Cynfor and 2) Arthur and March are first cousins. We are told Arthur and March son of Meirchion are first cousins in *The Dream of Rhonabwy* and in *Ystorya Trystan.*

Cynfor/Cunomorus/Chonomer was first identified with *'King Mark'* or March by the Breton monk Wrmonoc in his *Life of St. Paul of Leon*, written in 884. At some point Cunomorus/Cynfor was confused with the name Cynfarch. Cynfarch is from either **cintu-* (> W. *cyn*, *'former'*) or *cuno-* (perhaps in the sense of *'warrior'*) + *-march/-farch*, *'horse'*. There is also a hypothetical **cuno-* meaning *'high'*, thought to be found in Cunetio (Kennet, Wiltshire), Kent (Kenet, Cumbria) and Welsh Cynwyd (Merioneth, Wales).

In the past it has been supposed that Cunomorus/ Cynfor possessed, in addition to his British name, a Roman name Marcus. If this were so, it would adequately account for the Welsh form March.

However, *Kyn-/Cyn-* could also have been easily interpreted by someone with a rudimentary knowledge of English as OE *Cyne-*, a common proper name component. *Cyne-* means *'royal'* or *'kingly'*. A perceived *Cyne + march* could then have been wrongly be rendered as *'Royal or Kingly horse'*, i.e. King March.

So when Wrmonoc says, *'fama ejus regis Marci pervolat ad aures quemalio nomine Quonomorium vocant'*, "his [St. Paul Aurelian's] fame flew to the ears of King Marcus, known also as Cunomorus"*, he might well be mistranslating Cunomorus or, rather, Cynfarch, as *'King March'*.

Cynmarch or Cynfarch was the name of a famous cheiftain of the North. His father's name, Meirchion, just happens to match that of March's father:

- Cynfarch (or *King Mark*) son of Meirchion
- March son of Meirchion

It is my contention that the Welsh March son of Meirchion is an error for Cynmarch/Cynfarch son of Meirchion.

Similar errors have been made in other sources. One that comes to mind is Gildas's claim that Cuneglasus, in Latin, means *'Tawny Butcher'*. Cuneglasus actually means *'Bluish-Hound'*. The *superbo tyranno* of Gildas is generally regarded as pun on the name Vortigern, which does not mean *'Arrogant or Haughty Tyrant'*, but instead *'Over-lord'*. But it is just as possible Gildas was mistranslating the name Vortigern.

Geoffrey of Monmouth identified Cynfarch with Cunomorus. He calls the latter Chinmarchocus (variants Chinmarhogus, Chimarcous, Chinmarcus), i.e. Cynfarch, and makes him ruler of Treguier near Lannion in Brittany. A St. Tudwall founded the bishopric of Treguier and Cunomorus's father is said to have been one Tudwall. Kerduel near Lannion means *'Fort of Tudwall'*. Within the ancient diocese of Treguier stands the hill-fort Ruvarq or Run Marc'h, *'Mark's Hill'*, yet another site associated with Cunomorus as Mark.

In Britain, there is a Castellmarch near Abersoch on the Lleyn Peninsula in Gwynedd, Wales, and a Din Meirchion or *'Fort of Meirchion'* five miles from Henllan in Flintshire, only several miles South-East of the Moel Arthur hill-fort in the Clwydian Range. There are at least two traditional sites in Cornwall, one a Kilmarch not far from Lantyan and a Mark's Gate at Lantyan Wood.

In *The Dream of Rhonabwy*, March son of Meirchion leads the men of Llychlyn, usually a Welsh designation for Norway, but as Rachel Bronwich has shown, this is an error for Llydaw, the Welsh name for Brittany. As two stories are preserved on March in Gwynedd, and as there is a Llydaw in Gwynedd (Llyn Llydaw, *'Lake Llydaw'*), March's Llydaw in

The Dream of Rhonabwy could be either Gwynedd or Brittany.

Cynmarch/Cynfarch is better known as the father of Urien Rheged. It could well be this Cynfarch, mistakenly rendered '*King Mark*', who ruled from the Mote of Mark in Dumfries.

If we stick for the sake of argument with March, i.e. Cynfarch, as the first cousin of Arthur, then Uther would be the brother of Meirchion. With his nephew Cynfarch's fort in Dumfries, Uther himself must have ruled somewhere reasonably close by. The megalithic monument Long Meg and Her Daughters at Little Salkeld is sometimes called the Maughanby Circle. According to Ekwall, the early spellings of Maughonby preserve the Old Welsh personal name Meirchion. Thus is could be that Meirchion himself was from this region.

As Cynfarch's approximate birth date is c. 480 CE, and Arthur was his first cousin, this would make Arthur the perfect age to have fought in 513 CE at Badon and in 537 CE at Camlann.

This solution retains part of the Uther pedigree (Cynfor as '*Mark*', i.e. Cynfarch), while correcting for the chronological and geographical errors posed by Cynfor/Cunomorus and his successor Constantine, who were of a later period and from Cornwall and/or Brittany. When Cynfor was wrongly identified with Cynfarch/'*Mark*' of the North, Uther and Arthur, relatives of Cynfarch, were pulled into the Cynfor pedigree.

The father of Meirchion of the North is Gwrgwst Ledlum, father of Dyfnarth. This has been shown to be Fergus Mor, father of Domangart, the founder of Scottish Dalriada, who died c. 500 CE. This would give us part of our much needed explanation as to why all subsequent Arthurs are from Irish descended dynasties – especially the Dalriadan (see below). While the Welsh pedigree makes Ceneu son of Coel Hen of Strathclyde the father of Gwrgwst (as Ceneu heads most of the Northern dynasties), the real father of Fergus Mor was Erc/Eirc/Earca.

- Arthur son of Uther son of Fergus Mor of Dalriada

- Cynfarch son of Meirchion son of Fergus Mor of Dalriada

    Two versions of Fergus Mor's genealogy, which includes a late 6th century Arthur, run as follows:

- Artur son of Conaing son of Aedan son of Gabran son of Domangart son of Fergus
- Artur son of Aedan son of Gabran son of Domangart son of Fergus

We cannot say whether Gwrgwst/Fergus actually belongs in the Meirchion pedigree or if his name represents an intrusion into the British Northern genealogies. Certainly, Fergus's presence in the Meirchion pedigree is not an isolated instance. In the Strathclyde genealogy proper, we find a Garbaniaun son of [Ceneu son of] Coel Hen. This Garbaniaun has a son named Dumngual Moilmut or Dyfnwal Moelmul. Both names are, rather transparently, forms of the Dalriadan prince Gabran (Garbaniaun shows a metathesis of Gabran, plus a territorial suffix, as in Gwrtheyrniaun, a region named for Gwrtheyrn/Vortigern; cf. with Garban for Gabran in the Irish *Book of Lecan*) and his son Domnall. The Bran son of Dumngual/Domnall of the British pedigree is probably the attested Bran son of Aedan son of Gabran.

While we need not take these apparent intrusions of Irish Dalriadan royal names into the British Strathclyde genealogy at face value, they probably do indicate the existence of marriage ties between the Strathclyde Britons and their neighbors, the Dalriadans. Such marriage ties are hinted at in the records which pertain to the history of Scottish Dalriada.

Strathclyde, incidentally, was the kingdom of the ancient Damnonii or Dumnonii, a tribal group whose name is identical with that of the Dumnonii in southwestern Britain and the Domnonee in Brittany. The Arthur of southwest England is almost always associated with the territory of the Dumnonii.

We know of a 7th century Arthur son of Petuir of the Irish-founded dynasty in Dyfed. But there is some question as to whether this particular Arthur properly belongs in southwest Wales, or if his presence there indicates a relocation. Petuir, given that p and b commonly substitute for each other, and that t and c can often be mistaken for each other in MSS., looks to be the Bicoir, father of an Arthur who is situated in 7th century Kintyre of Dalriada.

I have offered as a possible explanation for the geographical dislocation of Bicoir (whose father is said to be a Briton) the fact that Kintyre or *Ceann - tir*, *'Head-land'* or *'Land's End'*, was confused at some point with Penbrog/Pembroke, *'Head-land'* or *'Land's End'*, in Dyfed, the centre of power in that kingdom. In *The Gododdin*, the Kintyre of Domnall Brecc grandson of Aedan son of Gabran is called *'pentir'*, which is the P-Celtic equivalent of the Q-Celtic Ceanntir.

There is another similarity as well. Both the Dyfed and Dalriadan dynasties list as their progenitors Eochaids. Eochaid or *'Horseman'* is cognate with the Latin equitis, *'knight'*. The Irish Deisi who came to Dyfed were led by the first of their dynasty, Eochaid Almuir. The Dalriadan Erc, father of Fergus Mor, was son of Eochaid Munremar. This Eochaid is believed by many to be a reflection of the Epidii or *'Horse-people'* tribe, who anciently inhabited Kintyre. We have seen how the Latin name Marcus became March in Welsh, a name meaning *'Horse'*. Meirchion, from L. Marcianus, may well have been associated with Welsh *meirch*, the plural of *march*.

Finally, we might compare the Dyfed genealogy of Arthur son of Petr/Petuir, which continues to Petuir's father Cyngar and thence to Voteporix, with the Northern Coel Votepauc genealogy, which passes down through Garbaniaun/Gabran, Dyfnwal/Domnall and Bran (son of Aedan) to Cyngar and Morgan Fwlch. The Votepo- of Voteporix is the same word as Votepauc, from an earlier Votepacos, meaning *'shelterer, protector, defender'*. I would suggest that it is to Coel Votepauc and the Cyngar of that line that Arthur son of Bicoir properly belongs.

Voteporix   Coel Hen Votepauc
                             [Dalriadans Gabran, Domnall
                             and Bran]

Cyngar	Cyngar
Petuir	Bicoir? and Morgan Fwlch
Arthur	Arthur?

Morgan Fwlch has been variously identified with the Morgan who killed Urien of Rheged or the Morgan who persecuted St. Kentigern on the Clyde. The precise location of his kingdom is uncertain, but it was definitely in the North, and probably in southwestern Scotland.

If I am right about Petuir = Bicoir, then all the known Arthurs either hail from or are related to the Northern British and Dalriadan dynasties.

FIGURE 4 - DUNRAGIT

We know nothing of the reign of Cynfarch, Meirchion's son, other than that he may have ruled from the Mote of Mark. But we do know a great deal about Urien of the next generation. He was a powerful king whose centre seems to have been Dunragit in Galloway, but whose battles and claimed territories extended to Strathclyde in the North, High

Rochester and Lindisfarne in the northeast, and Cattraeth in the south. His wife was named Modron, i.e. Matrona, the *'Divine Mother'* of the god Mabon (*'Divine Son'*) of Lochmaben, the Son's Ford at Ladyward and the Clochmabenstane in Dumfries. Modron's father was Afallach or Aballach, the Welsh cognate to Irish ablach, as in the Irish Otherworld Emhain Ablach, *'Emhain of the Apple Trees'*. In the context of Modron of Dumfries and northwestern Cumbria, Aballach should be seen as the eponymous god presiding over Aballava/Avalana/*'Avalon'*, the Roman fort at Burgh-By-Sands. I will have more to say on this fort in Chapter 7.

A curious line occurs in the early Welsh poem *Pa Gur*. There we are told that Mabon son of Modron is the servant of Uther Pendragon. While Mabon in a later Welsh story was identified with the youthful god Lleu of Gwynedd, the historical centre of Mabon worship, as already mentioned above, was in the North. The inscriptions we have from the Roman period place Mabon as Apollo Maponus at Corbridge (three altars), Ribchester (one shaft), Hadrian's Wall (an altar whose exact provenance is unknown) and Chesterholm (silver pendant). He is also attested at the Roman fort of Blatobulgium, now Birrens, between the Clochmabenstane and Lochmaben. Elsewhere, Welsh poetic tradition informs us that the Dumfries region was known as the *'country (gwlad) of Mabon'*.

Luguvalium, the ancient name for Carlisle, is derived from *Luguvalos*, supposedly a theonym meaning *'Lugus (or 'Lleu') – strong'* (cf. the Dinas Dinlleu fort in Arfon, Gwynedd, the *'Town of the Fort of Lleu'*). Alternately, this may have been the fort that was *'strong as Lugus'*. The proximity of this Luguvalos place-name to Lochmaben and the Clochmabenstane suggests that Lugus and Apollo Maponus of the North may have been identified with each other in a fashion similar to that of Lleu and Mabon of Gwynedd.

In passing, I would remind the reader of the presence of Loch Arthur between the town of Dumfries and the Mote of Mark, the hill of Arthur Seat just a few miles North-East of Longtown and another Arthur's Seat at 2376 ft elevation on Hart Fell.

In my book *The Secrets of Avalon*, I was able to show that while Arthur's mother Eigr (the correct Welsh form of Geoffrey of Monmouth's Latin Ygerna) is herself either a personification or goddess of the Tintagel headland, her association by the Welsh with Ercing in southereastern Wales is a reflection of her descent from Erc, the founder of Dalriada in Scotland.

The possibility that Arthur had a Dalriadan mother would provide us with another explanation for the apparent fact that all subsequent Dark Age Arthurs belonged to this region of the North. These men were named for the earlier, more famous Arthur whose mother was Dalriadan and whose father was British. The idea is lent support by the fact that, as we have seen, the Dalriadan royal line has *'intruded'* itself into the genealogies of the British kings of the North.

If the Dalriadans were related to the mother of Arthur, this may account for Aedan of Dalriada's battle at Degsastan. This place is believed to be Dawston in Liddesdale. We can surmise that after Arthur son of Uther died, perhaps without an heir, there arose a succession problem. Aedan pressed his claim, as Arthur was partly Dalriadan. However, it should be noted that Aedan's opponents at Dawston were English and there is no evidence of the British participating in the battle. It may be that there was a British-English alliance against Aedan or that the British had called in Aedan for help against the English.

If Arthur, then, belongs somewhere in southwestern Scotland or northwestern England, where exactly might we place him? And in what sense was he the chief war-leader in the North? To answer these questions, we next turn our attention to the battles of Arthur.

CHAPTER 3

THE BATTLES OF ARTHUR

THE FIRST BATTLE: AT THE MOUTH OF THE RIVER GLEIN

It has long been recognized that there are only two extant Glen rivers which conform philologically to *'Glein'* and which could have been subject to Saxon attack from the Continent in the 5th-6th centuries CE, the Age of Arthur. These are the Glen of Lincolnshire and the Glen tributary of the Till in Northumberland.

The Glen of Lincolnshire has no distinctive features or strategic fortifications which would make it of any value to an invading force. On the other hand, the Northumberland Glen is hard by the Yeavering Bell hill-fort, which prior to becoming a Saxon stronghold was the British Gefrin. Gefrin is from the Welsh word *gafr 'goat'* or a compound containing *gafr* plus Welsh *bryn* (mutated *fryn*), for *'Goat-hill'*. I would remind the reader, however, of a Gaulish god conflated with Mercury called Gebrinius. It is possible that Gefrin represents a British counterpart of this divine name.

The Yeavering Bell hillfort is 12.8 acres in size and encloses the two summits and the saddle between of a hill that rises to a height of 1181 ft above sea level. There is a single stone rampart 13 ft wide, with entrances midway along the north and south sides, and a third on the north-east. At the east and west ends are small, crescent-shaped annexes, the latter with an entrance at its mid-point. The centre of the fort was the site of about 130 circular huts. The eastern summit is ringed by a trench which held a wooden palisade nearly 164 ft in diameter. Archaeologists do not know whether there is any relationship between the hillfort and the Anglo-Saxon royal town of Ad Gefrin ('at Gefrin') that succeeded it at the foot of the hill.

FIGURE 5 - MOUTH OF THE RIVER GLEN

Other hill-forts abound in the region: Wooler, Kyloe Hills, Dod Law forts at Doddington, the Old Bewick hill fort and the Ros Castle fort and settlement between Chillingham and Hepburn. And, of course, the Roman road known as the Devil's Causeway, a branch off of Dere Street, passes only a couple of miles to the east of the mouth of the Glen.

Scholars who argue in favor of the Lincolnshire or 'Lindsey' Glen do so primarily because the following battle, that of the Dubglas, is put in a Linnuis region by the HB. Linnuis, as we will see, is wrongly thought to represent the later regional name Lindsey.

An actual battle at the mouth of the Lindsey or Lincolnshire Glen is scarcely possible, unless it were a battle of reconquest by Arthur and not a successful defensive engagement. This is because we have archaeological evidence for Saxon cemetaries well north, west and south of the Lindsey Glen as early as c. 475 CE.

The Next Four Battles: At The River Dubglas In The Linnuis Region

Philologists have long recognized that Old Welsh Linnuis must derive from Br.-Lat. *Lindensis, *Lindenses, or *Lindensia, and the identification with Lindsey works fine on purely linguistic grounds. Lindsey, of course, was the early English name for what we now think of as Lincolnshire.

The root of Lindensis is British *lindo-, 'pool, lake', now represented by Welsh llyn, 'pond, lake'. The Roman name for the town of Lincoln – Lindum – is from the same root. The 'pool' or 'lake' in question is believed to have been on the Witham River near the town.

The problem is that there is no Dubglas or 'Black Stream' (variants Douglas, Dawlish, Dowlish, Divelish, Devil's Brook, Dalch, Dulais, Dulas, etc.) in Lindsey. This has caused other place-name experts to situate the Dubglas battle either near Ptolemy's Lindum of Loch Lomond in Scotland or near Ilchester in Somerset, the Roman period Lindinis, as there are Dubglas rivers in both places. Unfortunately, neither of these candidates is satisfactory, because Arthur would not have been fighting Saxons at either location in the time period we are considering.

A site which has been overlooked, and which is an excellent candidate for Arthur's Dubglas, is the Devil's Water hard by the Hadrian's Wall fort of Corbridge, which has upon it a place called Linnels. Almost a century ago it was proposed that Linnels was from an unrecorded personal name. But modern place-name experts, upon looking at Linnels on the Ordnance Survey map, observed the remarkable double elbow in the Devil's Water with a lake nearby and concluded that Linnels was from a British *lindo-ol:in, "lake-elbow".

It was once thought that the Devil's Water stemmed from a Dilston Norman family, the D'Eivilles. But going by the earliest spelling of the Devil's Water (Divelis c. 1230) leads recent authorities to state uncategorically that this etymology is incorrect and the Devil's Water is certainly of the Dubglas river-name type.

The Devil's Water at Linnels is thus the only extant Dubglas river-name associated with a demonstrably Welsh lake-name that is geographically plausible as a battle site against Britons and Saxons during the period of Arthur.

Worth noting is the fact that the Roman Dere Street road at Corbridge splits immediately north of the Wall, the eastern branch or *'Devil's Causeway'* continuing North-NorthEast, straight to the Northumberland Glen.

As an aside, I would mention that the Battle of Hexham was fought at Linnels on May 14, 1464.

FIGURE 6 - THE DEVIL'S WATER AT LINNELS

THE SIXTH BATTLE: AT THE RIVER BASSAS

The Bassas river is the most problematic of the Arthurian battle sites, as no such stream name survives and we have no record other than this single instance in the HB of there ever having been a river so named. Conventional theory seeks to derive the first component of Bassas from W. *bas*, *'shallow'*. The suffix of this supposed bas river-name has so far eluded analysis, bringing up the possibility that Bassas itself is a corrupt form.

Bas or *'shallow'* is not found as a place-name component on the Continent or in Britain, nor even in Wales. We can only say that the location of the Bassas may be somewhere in the same general region as the Glen and Devil's Water battles. We will see below that the locations of subsequent battle sites will support this notion.

The fact that it is not recorded elsewhere suggests that *'shallow'* is not a particularly dramatic feature for a river of any significance and therefore it is not surprising that it was superseded by another more meaningful name. On the other hand, perhaps the battle occurred at a place where some (un-named) river was relatively shallow, a fairly wide, gravelly, slow-moving stretch of some river or other. Bassas would then mean *'the shallow place'*. That kind of one-off description need not have survived.

Some scholars have opted for a different origin for Bassas. They have pointed to Bass place names such as Bass Rock in the Firth of Forth, the Bass at Inverurie in Aberdeenshire and Bass Hill at Dryburgh.

Alas, the etymology for bass is fairly recent. In the *Scottish National Dictionary* there is an entry under *'bass'* as follows: *"A workman's tool basket; also a basket for carrying fish – known in Banff and Fife: on Lothian coast 'bass' is a square straw basket about 2' by 2' used for carrying fish."* Bass Rock and similar formations would have been named by fisher folk due to their resemblance to such a basket.

The Bass Burn or Bass *'stream'*, a tributary of the Scar or Scaur Water approximately 15 miles North-West of Dumfries and just south of Auchenhessnane, was originally called the Back Burn. Both the 1st edition (1861) and 2nd edition (1899) Ordnance Survey maps name it as Back Burn. The 1955 edition names it as Bass Burn. It is possible that either the original surveyors simply misheard what the local people called it, or that later surveyors did. As there are other Back Burns in Lowland Scotland, the chances that this stream's original name was Bass is slim.

A very acceptable explanation for the name Bassas is that it records an OE personal name found in place-names, i.e. Bassa. We find Bassingas or *'the people of Bassa'* in several placenames in England, but there are only two such places in Lowland Scotland/ Northumberland: Bassington at Cramlington and Bassington at Alnwick.

Bassington in Cramlington parish was a farmstead approximately 1½ miles north-west of the village. It appears on a map of 1769 and is probably a much older site. In the present day town of Cramlington the site of Bassington Farm is on the Bassington Industrial Estate. However, other than this Bassington's proximity to the Devil's Water at Linnels (approximately 20 miles as the crow flies), there is little to recommend it as the site of Arthur's Bassas River battle.

FIGURE 7 - THE RIVER ALN NEAR BASSINGTON

The *'tun of Bassa's people'* on the Aln is not far east of a Roman road that connects Dere Street and the Devil's Causeway. This Bassington is also roughly equidistant between the Northumberland Glen and the Devil's

Water/Dubglas near Hadrian's Wall, and near the Roman fort of Alauna on the Aln at Low Learchild.

The Alauna fort stands atop a slight rise with a fine view on all sides except where it is overlooked by the high ground about 1968 ft to the east. There is a *'bump'* in the occupation road which marks the northern rampart, and another in a hedge indicates the eastern limit of the fort. In the two fields to the east of the road the rampart is visible when viewed from a distance as a minor bank. The fields to the west of the road are regularly ploughed and so show no traces of the rampart. There are no surface indications in the fields south of the disused railway.

The east and north sides of two successive forts were revealed during investigations by I. A. Richmond. The earlier, contained within the other, was defended by two double ditches 8 feet wide and 8 feet apart, which had been deliberately filled with turf. The east side was at least 250 feet long and the north at least 130 feet long. The later fort had an east side at least 760 feet long and a north side at least 250 feet long. It was defended by a single ditch 15 feet wide and a clay rampart 23 feet wide.

If the battle of Bassas had been fought in the vicinity of Bassington, one of the streams in the vicinity of this tun may well have been referred to as *'Bassa's'* river.

The ending -*as* in Bassas has no explanation in either Latin or Welsh grammar. But it does have an explanation in Old English grammar. The name is thus probably Old English. Just as Baschurch (Shropshire) is from Old English *'Basses cirice'*, i.e. *'Basse's church'* (Eglwyseu Bassa in the Old Welsh poems), and Basford (Nottinghamshire) is Old English *'Basses ford'*, and Baslow Derbyshire) is Old English *'Basses hlaw'*, i.e. *'Basse's burial-mound'*; so *'flumen quod uocatur Bassas'* is easily understood as *'the river which is called Basse's'*, i.e. *'Basse's river'*. There is a Basingbourne in Cambridgeshire, Old English Basingeburna, which is *'the stream of Basse's people'*, *'Basse's kin's stream'*.

To argue that it makes no sense to have a Germanic name in the Arthurian battle list, I would only say this: for all we know, Arthur's opponent at the Bassas River may have been a chieftain named Bassa. If this were so, it is quite possible the British themselves would have referred to the river as Bassa's. Alternately, by the 9th century date of the HB, the old British name of the stream may have been forgotten, and it was only known that Arthur had fought at a river, which was now called Bassas.

One must imagine the Saxons coming up the Aln or its valley, with a mind towards reaching first the area of the Alauna fort and then continuing west on the connecting Roman road that branched off of the Devils' Causeway to meet up with Dere Street. The Devil's Causeway runs north from the Alauna fort, eventually passing just a little east of the mouth of the Glen, the location of Arthur's first battle.

THE SEVENTH BATTLE: THE CELIDON WOOD

Caledonia was originally the region of the Great Glen in Highland Scotland inhabited by the Caledonii. As such, in Classical usage Caledonia came to mean Scotland north of the Forth-Clyde isthmus. But in Welsh tradition - as is evidenced by the presence of Merlin at 1) Arthuret just north of Carlisle, 2) Drumelzier on the Tweed 3) the region near Glasgow), and 4) Eildon Mid Hill (= the Noquetran; see my study of Merlin in *The Secrets of Avalon*) - the Coed Celidon would appear to be at the heart of the Scottish Lowlands. It is generally accepted by scholars that this is indeed the location of the great wood in the Welsh sources.

We may be able to pinpoint the location of the Coed Celidon battle more precisely. Although Geoffrey of Monmouth has been justly criticized for producing stories of early British kings rather than histories, we cannot discount the possibility that at least occasionally his account of Arthur's reign may preserve accurate historical traditions. When he has Arthur face the Saxons in the Caledonian Wood, he tells us that *"Arthur... ordered the trees round that part of the [Caledonian] wood to be cut down and their trunks to be placed in a circle, so that every way out was barred to the enemy."* This is an odd statement, as one would expect such a palisade to be erected as a defensive structure and not one that is designed to contain the enemy.

The construction of a circular barrier in the Caledonian Wood brings to mind the semi-circular Catrail dyke of the Scottish Lowlands. The Catrail is a linear earthwork that runs from Robert's Linn to Hosecoteshiel and embraces the entire head of the Teviot basin from the Slitrig to beyond the Borthwick Water. It is not continuous, in the sense that is incorporates streams or woodland, and its engineering, in short sectors clumsily joined and imperfectly aligned, stamps it as a product of somewhat inexperienced communal effort. The date of its construction is doubtful, though it is usually thought to be English in origin. At least one authority thinks it might mark a political boundary established after Aethelfrith's victory at Degsastan (Dawston in Liddesdale) in 603 CE.

FIGURE 8 - THE CAPON OAK TREE IN WHAT WAS ONCE THE GREAT CALEDONIAN WOOD OF LOWLAND SCOTLAND

As the date of the construction of the Catrail is doubtful, could we not propose that it was built slightly earlier, say in the 6th century, the time of Arthur? The Catrail runs through what was the great Ettrick Forest, an extensive woodland stretching from Dumfriesshire to the Galashiels area.

The famous expert on Scottish place-names, William J. Watson, hypothesized that the ending of Catrail may be found in the stream-name Powtrail. The –ail of Powtrail has been shown to be Cumbric *eil, a wattle fence or woven hedge. In the poems of Taliesin, eil is used of any sort of construction involving plaiting or wattling and denoted a defensive construction. The word appears to be cognate with Irish aile, 'a fence'.

If the –ail of Catrail is 'fence', then, the first component is likely derived Gaelic cathair, 'fort'. Even though the medial th in cathair is silent (cf. W. caer, 'fort') and should not, formally speaking, have yielded Catr-, in Highland Scotland we do find the Brown and White Caterthun (cathair + dun) forts. If cathair could become cater in these names, certainly it could have become the Catr- of Catrail.

But if the Catrail is the 'Fort-fence', what fort are we talking about?

Scholars of linear earthworks in the Scottish Lowlands have brought the dyke into connection with the great North Eildon Hill fort of Trimontium.

Of the various earthworks in the Scottish Lowlands, only the Catrail seems likely to have functioned as a large scale territorial boundary. In association with other natural features, it may have functioned in respect of the hillfort of North Eildon Hill in the same role as the earthwork called 'The Dorsey' seems to have functioned in respect of the royal site of Emhain Macha in Ireland. It is now known that the Dorsey continued across bogland in the form not of a ditch, but of a palisade, and if such a feature was once incorporated into the design of the Catrail, the use of eil/ail, 'fence' for this feature would be apt.

The native fortification on Eildon North Hill was replaced by the Romans with their fort of Trimontium ('Three Mountains') at Newsteads. But the hill-fort itself was the largest in Scotland, being 39 acres in extent and occupying the summit of Eildon Hill North at an altitude of 1385 ft. Three phases of development have been distinguished, although the first two are somewhat difficult to trace on the ground.

In the first phase the fort included a small elliptical area on the highest part of the hill. Faint traces of the northern rampart may be seen, but it is much mutilated by later hut floors and on the southern side it is now represented only by a natural scarp.

In the second phase the whole of the summit plateau was enclosed; here again the defences are much wasted and are cut in two places by hut floors, but their line may be followed as a terrace on the North, West, and South, and as a slight rampart at the East end of the South side.

In the third phase the whole of the hill was enclosed by three ramparts and ditches. These survive mainly as terraces, but enough remains to reveal the plan, especially on the West side, where an internal quarry ditch is also visible. Four original entrances can be seen. No less than 296 hut floors have been identified within the fort and since most of these owe their survival to the fact that they are scooped out on slopes, the number should perhaps be doubled to allow for the more level areas.

Eildon North Hill is believed by most scholars to have been the oppidum of the Selgovae tribe.

It is reasonable to propose that the Catrail was the site of Arthur's battle within the Celidon Wood. The presumed Roman military road stretching from Torwood in Annandale to Raeburnfoot and thus to the Roman fort of Newsteads crossed the Catrail at some point. It is likely that Arthur reached the Catrail via this road and the battle itself could have taken place at this strategic juncture.

Obviously, we cannot discount the possibility that the story preserved in Geoffrey of Monmouth's account of the Celidon Wood battle may be anachronistic, in that the Catrail may post-date Arthur and he only later came to be associated with it in legend. We can be fairly certain, however, that the Celidon Wood was the great expanse of forest surrounding the Eildons. As Dere Street ran through this area to the south and north of Trimontium, and other Arthurian battles occur on or near Dere Street, another candidate for the location of this battle would be just to the east of the Eildons, rather than to the west of this triple hill.

THE EIGHTH BATTLE: THE CASTLE OF GUINNION

The Castle ('*Castellum*') Guinnion has been identified with the Roman fort of Vinovium at Binchester, although the great Professor Kenneth Jackson thought this unlikely. It has since been noted, however, that Ptolemy's alternative Vinnovium (B. **Uinnouion*) brings us very close to the later name set down by Nennius. Vinnovium should have given in Old Welsh at this stage a form in *–wy*, but it could be that *–ion* has been maintained as a so-called '*learned form*'. Thus the identification should not be rejected.

FIGURE 9 - BINCHESTER ROMAN FORT

Binchester is not far south of Hadrian's Wall on the Roman Dere Street. The fort stands on a spur of high ground some one and a quarter miles north of Bishop Auckland. It overlooks a loop in the river Wear and is in an excellent defensive position.

The fort was built in 79 CE during the Roman advance into northern England. From the early second century Binchester and the other Dere Street forts became important supply depots for Hadrian's Wall and developed as military centres controlling the region south of the Wall.

The fort was in continuous military use until the early years of the 5th century. After the final withdrawal of the garrison the fort and the surrounding vicus (civilian settlement) continued to be occupied by the local, native population and it would seem that Binchester remained an important small town. By the beginning of the 6th century the fort buildings were being torn down and stripped of stone. Part of the site was utilized by Anglo-Saxons as a cemetery.

THE NINTH BATTLE: THE CITY OF THE LEGION

The City of the Legion (*Urbs Legionis*) is, in this context, the Roman legionary fortress at York, the Romano-British Eburacum.

Dere Street began at the fort and ran north to Hadrian's Wall and beyond. The argument against York is that, according to Welsh sources, the only Roman forts called Cities of the Legion were Chester or Deva and Caerleon or Isca. But to claim the Welsh were ignoarant of the fact that York was a legionary fortress seems very doubtful. To begin, we have chieftains such as Peredur son of Efrauc (Efrauc = Eburacum/'York') and Peredur son of Eliffer (Eleutherius) Gosgordfawr. Peredur is a Welsh rendering of the Roman rank of Praetor. The governor or legate of Britannia Inferior, that is Northern Britain, was in the later period of praetorian rank.

The Roman emperor Caracalla reviewed the administration of Britain and split the province into two: Britannia Superior in the south, which had a consular governor based at London with two legions, the Twentieth at Chester and the Second at Caerleon. Britannia Inferior in the north had a praetorian governor with only one legion, the Sixth at York, where the governor also resided.

Peredur son of Eliffer is placed in two Northern battles. He is said to have been present at Arfderydd (Arthuret just north of Carlisle) and an unidentified Caer Greu or Fort Greu. Greu has been tentatively related to W. *creu*, *'blood'*. I would propose that Caer Greu/Creu is Carrawburgh, i.e. the Roman fort of Brocolitia, on Hadrian's Wall. English *'Carrawburgh'* could easily reflect something like very early Old Welsh **'Cair Carrou'*. The extant form of *'Caer Greu'* could be the regular Middle Welsh reflex of this.

FIGURE 10 - A LATER TOWER ERECTED ATOP THE FOUNDATION STONES OF ROMAN YORK

Eliffer the father of Peredur, by virtue of his son's name, would seem to have ruled from York. If so, then his epithet Gosgordfawr may be significant. It means *'[of the] Great Retinue'*. Could not this *'great retinue'* of a ruler of York - a ruler whose son's name means *'praetor'* – be a memory of the York legion?

The Romans constructed their first fort at Eboracum in 71 CE. The fort's rectangular construction consisted of a V-shaped ditch and earthen ramparts with a timber palisade, interval towers and four gateways. It covered about 50 acres of a grid-plan of streets between timber barrack blocks, storehouses and workshops. More important buildings included the huge Principia (Headquarters Building), the Commandant's House, a hospital and baths. The fort was designed to house the entire legion and remained a military headquarters almost to the end of Roman rule in Britain.

The fortifications at York were strengthened around 80 CE by a caretaker garrison while the Ninth Legion campaigned with the governor, Julius Agricola, in Wales and Scotland. The original fort was replaced in 108 CE by a massive stone structure with walls that survived long enough to be incorporated into the defenses of Viking and even later medieval York.

THE TENTH BATTLE: THE SHORE OF THE RIVER TRIBRUIT

The location of the shore (W. *traeth*) of the river Tribruit has remained unresolved. The clue to its actual whereabouts may lie in the two possible meanings assigned to this place-name. According to Kenneth Jackson, Tribruit, W. *tryfrwyd*, was used as an adjective, meaning *'pierced through'*. His rendering of traeth tryfrwyd was *'the Strand of the Pierced or Broken (Place)'*. Basing his statement on the Welsh Traeth Tryfrwyd, Jackson said that *"we should not look for a river called Tryfwyd but for a beach."* However, Jackson later admitted that *"the name (Traith) Tribruit may mean rather 'The Many-Coloured Strand'*. Most recently traeth tryfrwyd has been defined as either the *"very speckled shore"* (try- here being the intensive prefix *tri-, cognate with L. *trans*) or the shore *"bespattered [with blood]."*

However, it is worth pointing out that the 'tryfrwyd' which means 'very speckled' and the 'tryfrwyd' which means 'piercing, pierced' are the same word, and that the latter is the historically primary meaning. The meaning 'very *speckled'* comes through *'blood-stained'* from *'pierced'*, something being *'blood-stained'* because it was *'pierced'* in battle.

In other words, the original meaning of the word is *'pierced-through'*.

That *'pierced'* or *'broken'* is to be preferred as the meaning of Tribruit is plainly demonstrated by lines 21-22 of the *Pa Gur* poem:

Neus tuc manauid - Manawyd(an) brought

Eis tull o trywruid - pierced ribs (or, metaphorically, 'timbers') from Tryfrwyd

Tull, *'pierced'*, here obviously refers to Tribruit as *'through-pierced'*.

In the poem, the shore of Tryfrwyd battle is listed one just prior to Din Eidyn and once just after the same fort (I will have more on the *Pa Gur* battle sites below). The Gwrgi Garwllwyd or *'Man-dog Rough-grey'* who is also placed at Tryfrwyd has been associated with the Cynbyn or *'Dog-heads'* Arthur fought at Din Eidyn.

Manawyd's role at Tryfrwyd may suggest that this river or its shore is to be found in or on the borders of Manau Gododdin, which was the district round the head of the Firth of Forth, whose name remains in Slamannan and Clackmannan. The Fords of Frew west of Stirling have been proposed as the site of the battle, but Jackson claims W. *frut* or *ffrwd*, *'stream'*, cannot have yielded *frwyd*. Jackson also countered Skene's theory that this was the Forth, on the grounds that the Welsh name for the Forth, Gweryd, which would be **Guerit* in OW.

The poem may be even more specific, in that Traeth Tryfrwyd is said to be *'ar eidin cyminauc'* (line 28), *'at Eidyn on the border'*. Now, the *'border'* here could be the Firth of Forth, but it is much more likely to be the line of division between Gododdin proper and Manau Gododdin.

The Cynbyn or *'Dog-heads'* may partly owe their existence to the Coincenn daughter of Aedan, father of the Dalriadan Arthur, and to the Coinchend in the Irish story *The Adventure of Art son of Conn*. In this Irish tale, Art battles a monstrous woman named Coincenn or *'Dog-head'* who is a member of a tribe bearing the same name.

The name of Art son of Conn's mother may be significant in this context. She was called Eithne, which was also the name of the mother of the god Lugh. The place-name Eidyn is of unknown etymology. Because Din Eidyn was the capital of Lothian, and Lothian is derived from Middle Welsh Lleudinyawn, Brittonic **Lugudunia:non*, land of *'Lugh's (W. Lleu's) Fortress'*, it would be reasonable to suggest that Eidyn as Lugh's fortress represents a British form of Irish Eithne. Din Eidyn would then be the Fort of (the goddess) Eithne.

The Coincenn of the Irish are thought to be a reflection of the Classical Cynacephali.

While these mythical elements may have continued the the Dog-head theme in the Tribruit battle, I believe there to be an actual historical foundation for this group of canine warriors. Just north of the Forth and Manau Gododdin was an ancient tribe called the Venicones. As Welsh b could substitute for v in some cases (the name Bran, for instance, can be found as Vran), a Beni-cones may well have been interpreted, either fancifully or through error, as Cyn-byn. If so, then the Cynbyn Arthur is supposed to have fought on the border of Eidyn would have been the Venicones.

As for the *'Pierced/Broken-Through Shore'* itself, I would mention Broken Hook, which lay by the river Avon. Hook is either from OE hoc, *'bend in a river'*, or from a possible **huc*, *'river-bend'*. Broken Hook is found as brokenheugh in 1551 and describes a place where a natural break-through has occurred in a river bend. The history of the nearby River Carron demonstrates that breakthroughs in the meanders did occur.

Broken Hook was one of the pendicles of the barony of Abbotskerse. It can be found in five charters relating to that entity plus one further one in a post-Reformation retour. There are no overt references to its location but on two occasions it appears thus: 1587 Brokinheuk et Reddoch; 1635 Brokinhouk et Ridheuch. It is this association with Reddoch that prompts us to locate it on the Avon rather than the Carron.

Reddoch was described in 1749:

"--- all and haill these nine oxengates of Redheugh with houses [etc] with also the fishings upon the Water of Avon --- and also these parts [glosses particatas (anglice) lie falls] ultra Gramma Salsa (anglice lie Salt Grass) called Henry Hooks Saltgrass and lie Hooks Saltgrass --- said lands of Redheugh omnium per prius mixtarum (anglice Runrig)".

FIGURE 11 - THE AVON NEAR BROKEN HOOK

It is possible that the last of these two, Hooks Saltgrass, might relate to the lost Broken Hook and might be for Broken Hook's Saltgrass.

These names relate to saltings on the tidal parts of the rivers. There must be an even stronger suspicion that the place named Hook on an estate plan of 1806 may be the lost Broken Hook in view of its location. The last should not be confused with Heuk which lay on the east bank of the River Carron at its confluence with the Forth.

Broken Hook at Reddoch was just a little north of Inveravon, the *'Mouth of the Avon'*, at the Antonine Wall, with its temporary Roman camps.

The first two camps at Inveravon were discovered from the air in the mid-1950's. They lie close to the east end of the Antonine Wall, 1,750 ft south of the Wall and a half mile south-east of Inveravon. The third camp was found on aerial photographs in 1960 on a southward slope 400 ft south of the Wall.

The 8 acre Inveravon Camp 1 is aligned north-south with gateways in the centre of the east and west sides, the latter protected by an external ditch. The 1.25 acre Camp 2 lies across the southern part of this camp and extends towards the edge of the Esk escarpment. Camp 3, 7 acres in size, lies close to the wall just north-west of Camps 1 and 2.

Only a few miles to the east of Broken Hook is the Roman fort at Carriden. The fort of Carriden is at the eastern terminus of the Antonine Wall. This name is thought to represent an earlier Caer Eidyn. But even if so, Carriden as a designation for this fort would appear to be relatively late, as at an earlier time it was called 'End of the Wall' [Penguaul, Cenail, Peneltun], a descriptive term later applied to neighboring Kinneil. The Roman period name of the fort was Velunia or Veluniate.

Some scholars think that Carriden and other Roman forts in the region formed a chain of defences along the Lothian shore of the Firth of Forth. This idea is sound, as it would mirror the situation at the western end of Hadrian's Wall, where the 'Western Sea Defences' are composed of a series of forts and watchtowers along the coast of Cumbria.

Aerial photographs of Carriden reveal three ditches, forming the defences of the east and part of the south side. The east side was some 440 ft long, and contained a gate 150 ft from the south-east angle ; the length of the south rampart appears to have been at least 400 ft. The western half of the fort lies within the grounds of Carriden House, while even such part of the site as is available for digging seems to have been heavily denuded.

The headwaters of the Avon are at Slamannan or Sliabh Manau, the 'Hill of Manau', and this river empties into the Firth of Forth at the eastern terminus of the Antonine Wall in Manau Gododdin. The Carron is also in Manau Gododdin. I would identify the Traeth Tribruit, the *'Broken Shore'*, with Broken Heugh, the *'Broken River-Bend'* at the mouth of the Avon.

A NOTE ON THE DALRIADAN ARTHUR'S DEATH FIGHTING THE MIATHI

Before leaving this discussion of Arthur's battle at the Tribruit, we should briefly consider its significance in the context of the the death of the Dalriadan Arthur, son of Aedan, while fighting the Miathi.

As it turns out, we know that part of the Miathi tribal area appears to have roughly corresponded with Manau Gododdin. We have two extant place-names featuring the name of this tribe, which was known as the Maeatae in the Roman period: the Myot Hill fort 2 miles west of Denny and the Dumyat hill-fort 2.5 miles east of Bridge of Allan.

The Dalriadan Arthur's death is also placed in Circenn. This has created a major problem, for Circenn is the Pictish province lying to the north of the Firth of Tay and this is quite a distance from the territory of the Miathi. Scholars have tried to account for this confusion over the battle site location in various ways.

As none have been able to properly place the Tribruit battle – which would appear to have been within the Miathi region – the notion that two Arthurs may have been involved did not occur to anyone. It could be, for instance, that the earlier British Arthur fought a battle at Broken Hook on the Avon in Miathi territory, while the later Dalriadan Arthur died fighting in Circenn. However, we will see below (Chapter 4) that the British Arthur may have been placed on the border of Circenn in an early poem, casting doubt on his participation in either of the battles.

While I would like to believe that the British Arthur truly belongs at Broken Hook, his other northern-most battles – those at the mouth of the Glen, at the stream near Bassington and even at the Catrail in the Ettrick Forest – are well south of the Avon River. In fact, the Glen, Bassas and Celidon Wood battles form a rough line just south of the

Tweed. This strongly suggests that the British Arthur was not fighting anywhere north of that river. Instead, he was concentrating his efforts in the region that would later become the nucleus of English Bernicia.

THE ELEVENTH BATTLE: MOUNT AGNED

Mount Breguoin has been associated with the *'cellawr Brewyn'* or cells of Brewyn where Urien of Rheged later fought, a site generally agreed to be the Roman fort of Bremenium at High Rochester on Dere Street. Kenneth Jackson came to this conclusion. Most scholars now think that the Breguoin battle was taken from the Urien poem and incorporated into the Arthurian battle-list in the HB.

Mount Agned has hitherto escaped philological analysis. From Kenneth Jackson's time on, one original form proposed has been Angned. But this is an unknown word and has failed to produce a viable site. Most authorities feel that Agned is a corruption.

The simplest explanation for Agned as a corrupt form has been supplied by Dr. Andrew Breeze of the University of Navarre. Dr. Breeze proposes as a textual emendation for Agned as MW *agued*. The n > u copying error is a common one.

The word *agued* is a rare one, and is used only three times in the early materials. It means something like *'dire straits, difficulty, anxiety'*.

The most important use of this word, for the present purpose, is found in *Canu Aneirin* line 1259, where it occurs in the phrase *'twryf en agwed'*, *'a host in dire straits'*. We will return to this phrase in a moment.

We have discussed the possibility that the Arthur section in HB represents a Latin retelling of an OW heroic poem. Such a poem could have had a line in it like *'galon in agued'*, *'the enemy in dire straits, great difficulty'*, much like the *Canu Aneirin's 'twryf en agwed'*. It is conceivable that an author responsible for the Harleian recension of the HB (who may not have been entirely versed in the diction of OW heroic poetry) may have mistaken this *'agued'* for a actual place-name, and wrongly placed the battle there: instead of *'the enemy in dire straits'*, he understood *'the enemy at Agued'*, easily miscopied at some point as *'Agned'* as Breeze suggests.

FIGURE 12 - HIGH ROCHESTER ROMAN FORT

Under this interpretation, the only location for the battle that was ever correct was Breguoin/Bremenium. This analysis at least solves the problem of *'Where was Agned?'* with the answer, *'There never was such a place, and so no need to look for it.'*

What we may have in *'Mount Agued'*, then, is a confused reference to a battle at Mount Breguoin/Bremenium where the enemy found itself *'in dire straits'*. If so, we would have four, and possibly five battles having been fought by Arthur on Dere Street: York, Binchester, Devil's Water, Celidon Wood and High Rochester.

The argument against Bremenium/High Rochester as an Arthurian battle, which relies upon the presence of gellawr brewyn, the *'cells of Bremenium'*, in the Urien battle poem list, ignores the very real possibility that more than one battle could have been fought at Bremenium at different times. Bremenium is situated in a very strategic position, essentially guarding the pass over which Dere Street crosses the Cheviots. It is also true that Urien's Brewyn could just as easily have been borrowed from the Arthurian battle-list as the other way around.

While it may well be that Agued/Agned is merely an error for Bregouin or a poetic name for the latter, there is a second and perhaps better identification for this Arthurian battle site. The 'Twryf yn aguedd' phrase mentioned above comes from the 'Gwarchan Tudfwlch', a poem appended to *The Gododdin*.

What is surprising about the 'Gwarchan Tudfwlch' example is that the phrase is preceded by two lines that copy part of a line found in Strophe 25 of *The Gododdin* proper:

> "*Arf anghynnull,*
>
> *Anghyman ddull,*
>
> *Twryf en agwed...*"
>
> "*Arf anghynnull, anghyman ddull...*"

Now, in the case of *The Gododdin* line, the poet Aneirin is referring to Graid son of Hoywgi's prowess at the disastrous battle of Catraeth, Roman Cataractonium, modern-day Catterick on Dere Street in Yorkshire. The Battle of Catraeth is, of course, the subject of *The Gododdin* poem.

The hero Tudfwlch hailed from the region of Eifionydd in Gwynedd, but he fought and died at Catraeth. While he engaged in military actions in his homeland (the 'Gwarchan's' 'Dal Henban' is almost certainly modern Talhenbont at Llanystumdwy in Eifionydd), it is probable that the lines borrowed from *The Gododdin* are meant to indicate that the following 'Twryf yn angwedd', 'a host in distress', is a reference to the British army at Catraeth. Dr. Isaac Graham of The National University of Ireland, Galway, agrees with me on this assessment, saying that

> "*Phrases like twryf yn aguedd are characteristically used in early Welsh poetry to set up a general atmosphere of warrior violence, but, to judge from the*

final lines of the poem, it would seem to be primarily concerned with the 'Battle of Catraeth'."

Part of the Roman fort at Catterick was built on the rising ground above the River Swale known as Thornbrough Hill. And Arthur is mentioned in Line 972 of *The Gododdin.* Whether this is an interpolation or not, it is generally thought to be one of the earliest occurrences of his name in the written records:

> *"He fed black ravens on the rampart of a fortress*
>
> *Though he was no Arthur.*
>
> *Among the powerful ones in battle, In the front rank, Gwawrddur was a palisade."*

FIGURE 13 - THORNBROUGH HILL, CATTERICK

Are we to see as a coincidence Arthur's being mentioned in the context of the Battle of Catraeth when it is in this same battle, alone among all battles of the period, that a host finds itself in *'agued'?* I think not.

There are two possible ways to read this passage on Arthur in *The Gododdin.* First, the hero Gwawrddur, while a great warrior, was not nearly as great as Arthur. This is the standard interpretation. But let us suppose that what is really meant is that Arthur had fought at Catterick as well, a generation earlier, only he proved more powerful than

Gwawrddur and won a victory over the Saxons on Thornbrough Hill, i.e. Mount Agned.

In this context, the Arthurian Mount Agned of the HB is an anachronistic reference to the hill at Cataractonium, where the British army of Gwawrddur's time found itself in *'distress'* or *'dire straits'* just prior to its annihilation by the Saxon foe.

So where did Arthur fight – at High Rochester or Catterick? Well, the simple answer is *'Either, both or neither.'* If Breguoin is indeed borrowed from the *Urien* poem, then Arthur did not fight at High Rochester. If Agned is Thornborough Hill at Catterick, then the site may have been chosen merely because his name was mentioned in *The Gododdin.*

Almost the entire defensive circuit of the High Rochester/Bremenium fort is preserved, with the remains of the western gateway being particularly fine. There is also evidence of several periods of rebuilding in the western interval-tower of the south side. The ditches are well preserved to the north and east, outside which the line of Dere Street marches north-west.

Between the thick stone ramparts the fort measures around 440 ft north-south by about 420 ft east-west, giving an occupation area of about 4.25 acres. There are inner stone buildings. On the north, the remains of as many as thirteen ditches can be distinguished. On the east and south, four, and six ditches curve around the north-west angle. It is unknown how many ditches were on the west side of the fort.

The Roman fort at Catterick was likely founded during the early 70 CE's to guard the crossing of Dere Street over the River Swale. At the very latest, the fort must have been in place by 79 CE, in order to guard the northern supply route of Agricola's Scottish campaigns. After an undetermined period of neglect, it would appear that the fort was recommissioned during the administration of Gnaeus Julius Verus in the aftermath of the Brigantian revolt of 155 CE, at which time the Antonine Wall was abandoned and the troops pulled back to Hadrian's Wall in order to control the

Brigantes. No trace of the fort remains, as it was overlain by the town of Catterick. A crop-mark east of Catterick Racecourse has been identified as a Roman temporary camp not far from the fort.

THE TWELFTH BATTLE: MOUNT BADON

Badon is a difficult place-name for an unexpected reason: as Kenneth Jackson proclaimed: *"No such British name is known, nor any such stem."*

Graham Isaac has the following to say on the nature of the word Badon, which I take to be authoritative. His explanation of why Gildas's Badon cannot be derived from one of the Badburys (like Liddington Castle, often cited as a prime candidates for Badon) is critical in an eventual identification of this battle site. Although long and rather complicated, his argument is convincing and I have, therefore, opted to present it unedited:

> *"Remember in all that follows that both the -d- in Badon and the -th- in OE Bathum are pronounced like th in 'bathe' and Modern Welsh -dd-. Remember also that in Old English spelling, the letters thorn and the crossed d are interchangeable in many positions: that is variation in spelling, not in sound, and has no significance for linguistic arguments.*
>
> *It is curious that a number of commentators have been happy to posit a 'British' or 'Celtic' form Badon. The reason seems to be summed up succinctly by Tolstoy in the 1961 article (p. 145): 'It is obviously impossible that Gildas should have given a Saxon name for a British locality'. Why? I see no reason at all in the world why he should not do so (begging the question as to what, exactly, is the meaning of 'British locality' here; Gildas is just talking about a hill). This then becomes the chief crutch of the argument, as shown on p. 147 of Tolstoy's article: 'But that there was a Celtic name 'Badon' we know from the very passage in Gildas under discussion'.*
>
> *But that is just circular: ' "Badon" must be "Celtic" because Gildas only uses "Celtic" names'. This is no argument. What would have to be shown is that 'Badon' is a regular reflex of a securely attested 'Celtic'*

word. This is a matter of empirical detail and is easily tested; we have vast resources to tell us what was and was not a 'Celtic' word. And there is nothing like 'Badon'. So what do we do? Do we just say that 'Badon' must be Celtic because Gildas uses it? That gets us nowhere.

So what of the relationships between aet Bathum - Badon - Baddanbyrig? The crucial point is just that OE Bathum and the Late British / very early Welsh Badon we are talking about both have the soft -th- sound of 'bathe' and Mod.Welsh 'Baddon'. Baddanbyrig, however, has a long d-sound like -d d- in 'bad day'. Both languages, early OE and Late British, had both the d-sound and the soft th-sound. So:

1) If the English had taken over British (hypothetical and actually non-existent) *Badon (*Din Badon or something), they would have made it *Bathanbyrig or the like, and the modern names of these places would be something like *Bathbury.

2) If the British had taken over OE Baddanbyrig, they would have kept the d-sound, and Gildas would have written 'Batonicus mons', and Annales Cambriae would have 'bellum Batonis', etc. (where the -t- is the regular early SPELLING of the sound -d-; always keep your conceptions of spellings and your conceptions of sounds separate; one of the classic errors of the untrained is to fail to distinguish these). I imagine if that were the case we would have no hesitation is identifying 'Baton' with a Badbury place.

But the d-sound and the soft th-sound are not interchangeable. It is either the one or the other, and in fact it is the soft th-sound that is in 'Badon', and that makes it equivalent to Bathum, not Baddanbyrig.

(That applies to the sounds. On the other hand there is nothing strange about the British making Bad-ON out of OE Bath-UM. There was nothing in the Late British/early Welsh language which corresponded to the dative plural ending -UM of OE, so it was natural for the Britons to substitute the common British suffix -ON for the very un-British OE suffix -UM: this is not a substitution of SOUNDS, but of ENDINGS, which is quite a different matter. That Gildas then makes an unproblematic Latin adjective with -icus out of this does not require comment.)

To conclude:

1) There is no reason in the world why a 6th-century British author should not refer to a place in Britain by its OE name.

2) There was no 'British' or 'Celtic' *Badon.

3) 'Badon' does not correspond linguistically with OE Baddanbyrig.

4) 'Badon' is the predictably regular Late British / early Welsh borrowing of OE Bathum.

Final note: the fact that later OE sources occasionally call Bath 'Badon' is just a symptom of the book-learning of the authors using the form. Gildas was a widely read and highly respected author, and Badon(-is) (from Gildas's adjective Badon-icus) will quickly and unproblematically have become the standard book-form (i.e. primarily Latin form) for the name of Bath. Again, all attempts to gain some sort of linguistic mileage from the apparent, but illusory, OE variation between Bathum and Badon are vacuous."

It is thus safe to say that *'Badon'* must derive from a Bath name. However, we must not restrict ourselves to the Southern Bath, which makes no sense in the context of a Northern Arthur. For as it happens, there is a major Northern *'Bath'* site that has gone completely unnoticed.

In the the High Peak District of Derbyshire we find Buxton. This town had once been the southermost part of Brigantian tribal territory. In the Roman period, Buxton was the site of Aquae Arnemetiae, *'the waters in front of (the goddess) Nemetia'.* To the best of our knowledge, Bath in Somerset and Buxton in Derbyshire were the only two *'Aquae'* towns in Britain.

But even better, there is a Bathum name extant at Buxton. The Roman road which leads to Buxton from the northeast, through the Peak hills, is called Bathamgate. Batham is *'baths'*, the exact dative plural we need to match the name Bathum/Badon. *-gate* is *'road, street'*, which comes from ME *gate*, itself a derivative of OScand *gata*. Bathamgate is thus *'Baths Road'*.

The recorded forms for Bathamgate are as follows:

- *Bathinegate (for Bathmegate), 1400, from W. Dugdale's Monasticon Anghcanum, 6 vols, London 1817-1830.*

- *Bathom gate, 1538, from Ancient Deeds in the Public Record Office*

- *Batham Gate, 1599, from records of the Duchy of Lancaster Special Commissions in the Public Record Office.*

Buxton sits in a bowl about one thousand feet above sea level surrounded by mountains and is itself a mountain spa. The natural mineral water of Buxttom emerges from a group of springs at a constant temperature of 82 degrees Fahrenheit and is, thus, a thermal water. There are also cold springs and a supply of chalybeate (iron bearing) water. The evidence of Mesolithic man suggests a settlement dating to about 5000 BCE and archaeological finds in the Peak District around the settlement show habitation through the Neolithic, Bronze and Iron Ages to the time of the Romans. From the historical evidence we can say that Buxton was a civilian settlement of some importance, situated on the intersection of several roads, and providing bathing facilities in warm mineral waters. In short, it was a Roman spa. Place-names in and around Buxton, and Anglo-Saxon finds in burial mound excavations, suggest a continuing inhabitation of the area and probable use of the mineral waters.

It has long been speculated that we should expect to find a military installation at Buxton. However, subsequent archaeological fieldwork, including excavations, in and around suggested locations at the spa town have singularly failed to establish a military presence. A *'ditch feature'* identified initially through resistivity survey and then from aerial photography above Mill Cliff, Buxton, gave rise to the almost confident interpretation of this site as being that of the fort: subsequent evaluation in advance of development however has shown that these features were geological rather than man-made, and the absence of Roman finds of any description from a series of evaluation trenches suggests that if Buxton had a fort it was located elsewhere.

Today, the site of the probable Roman baths is covered by the Georgian Crescent building. In this area during the seventeenth and eighteenth century discoveries of lead lined baths, red plaster and building remains were made at some considerable depth in the sediments which surround the area of St Anne's well. In the eighteenth century, Pilkington investigated a mound overlooking the site of the previous discoveries. Here he found a structure which has been interpreted as a probable classical temple - one of only three known from Britain. In the mid-seventies, following the removal of a 20th century swimming pool, a brick structure was exposed and a deposit containing 232 Roman coins, 3 bronze bracelets and a wire clasp ranging in date from the 1st to the end of the 4th century CE was excavated.

This intriguing series of early discoveries lends tangible support to the interpretation of Buxton as the *'Bath of the North'*, but the character and extent of civilian settlement - and whether this was in association with a military installation or not, remains obscure. A considerable range of small finds, together with occasional glimpses of apparently Roman contexts, from the backgardens of houses has failed to provide a clear sense of the extent of Roman Buxton, let alone a soundly based understanding of its chronology and development. The dating of coinage in the 'votive' deposit from near the Crescent might be seen to indicate heightened frequencies of offerings during the third and fourth centuries. To what extent this might correlate with the development of settlement at Buxton is a matter of some conjecture.

FIGURE 14 - ST. ANNE'S WELL AT BUXTON

At Poole's cavern, Buxton, excavations between 1981 and 1983 by Peakland Archaeological Society and Buxton Archaeological Society produced a large Romano-British assemblage containing a considerable body of metalwork including coins and brooches, rolls of thin sheet bronze, along with ceramics, a faunal assemblage and burials. The dating of the coins and fibulae point to use between the late 1st and 3rd centuries, with the majority being of 2nd century date. Indeed, reanalysis of the material has suggested that the cave saw its principal period of use between 120 and 220 CE. The excavators appeared to reveal some spatial separation of the coin and fibulae finds from the pottery and faunal remains, although this has been questioned. Discussing the possible character of the use of the site Bramwell and Dalton draw attention to the comparative absence of spindle whorls, loom weights and bone hairpins which might be expected from a domestic site. Instead, they see the evidence as supporting the interpretation of the site as that of a rural shrine or sanctuary. This too has subsequently been questioned and rejected. Instead, Branigan and Dawley interpret the site as essentially domestic, but with the additional refuse from a metalworker's activities. They see a link between Poole's Cavern and the growth of Buxton as a spa centre providing a ready local market for small decorative trinkets.

A detailed listing of the baths discovered at Buxton:

- *Red bath: The wall surrounding St. Anne's Well prior to 1709*

- *Lead bath: Discovered in driving a sough in 1695*

- *The great bath: Discovered in driving a sough in 1695*

- *The plaster bath: Discovered during the construction of the Crescent*

- *The small bath: Discovered during the construction of the Crescent*

- *The Salt Bath: Discovered in 1883*

And the probable date ranges of these baths:

THE RED BATH

Size: 3' by 3'.

Date: Roman or late medieval/early post-medieval.

Location: Destroyed by Delves? Site probably destroyed by the west wing of the Crescent.

The wall surrounding the earlier St. Anne's Well, which lay under the present St. Anne's Hotel, is variously described as being covered in hard red cement, or being built in brick.

The hard red cement could be a description of a typical Roman construction technique involving the use of pounded tile, as could the use of brick. Gibson's Camden describes the material in 1722 as *'red Roman Plaister'*. Brick was in use both in the Roman period and from the late medieval period onwards in this region. It is not inconceivable that this wall dates from the later period. Pearson records that in digging the foundation for Delves' replacement well remains of a *'magnificent Roman structure'* were encountered.

LEAD BATH

Discovered in driving a sough in 1695.

Size: 6' by 6' by 1' deep, or 12' by 12' and probably 3' deep.

Date: Probably Roman.

Location: Under roadway in front of Crescent: '100yds along Whites' sough' or '50 yds East of Delves' alcove'.

The materials and form of this bath suggest, by analogy, a Roman date. The majority of the Roman baths at Bath appear to have had a lead lining and to have been constructed in a similar fashion. The small size (6 by 6) suggests that rather than being a bath, this was probably, either some form of reservoir, which sources suggest was fed from Bingham Well, or part of a bath house suite. Found at a depth of 12'.

THE GREAT BATH

Discovered in driving Whites' sough in 1695.

Size: 60' by 21' by 6' deep.

Date: Roman or Medieval

Location: Under roadway in front of Crescent: found along Whites' sough.

This is smaller than the Great Bath at Bath (72' by 29') but larger than the secondary Lucas Bath (43' by c20'). This is made of stone with smooth sides, and found at a depth of 6'.

THE PLASTER BATH

Discovered during the construction of the Crescent.

Size: 30'(East-West) by 15' by 3'+ deep.

Date: Roman or medieval.

Location: Not known with precision: 6 yds from the natural baths?

The width is in keeping with the natatio bath at Bath but it is some 9' shorter. This rough limestone bath had a spring and a floodgate and was lined with plaster and topped with wooden beams. Pilkington's description of the construction method suggests rubble set in mass mortar, which is a specifically Roman trait. Later descriptions claim the lining contained pounded tiles which if correct again suggests a Roman date. Denman spoke to the workmen who discovered this bath and says all that was discovered was a rudely built room with stone steps, small pieces of red plaster and timbers. Pearson records that this contained bottles that might be Roman. The mention of the bottles and Denman's description could suggest that this site might be the remains of some later medieval structure, perhaps even the chapel.

THE SMALL BATH

Discovered during the construction of the Crescent.

Size: Unknown.

Date: Unknown.

Location: Not known with precision.

Stone walled.

THE SALT BATH

Discovered in 1883.

Location: Outside study area.

Bray records the discovery of the corner of a building constructed of squared stone during the digging of Crescent foundations near a newly discovered warm spring. No other details are known.

The general trend of the evidence suggests that the Roman site may have consisted of a temple overlooking a set of Roman baths. At Bath we have a clear idea of the layout of a significant bath/water shrine complex which consisted of two major ranges: a temple and a religious precinct, within which lay the sacred spring; alongside this range were a line of three baths within a major building, at one end of which lay a typical Roman bathhouse or sauna. The Bath buildings were lavishly built in a classical style and the whole complex attracted visitors from outside the province.

In essence the Buxton layout mirrors that a Bath: parallel to the spring line is a temple and alongside the springs is a range of possibly Roman baths. As the Buxton temple is two-thrids the size of that at Bath we could assume the Buxton complex was somewhat smaller.

If the grove of the goddess Nemetia continued as an important shrine well into Arthur's time (and the presence of St. Anne's Well at the site of the town's ancient baths shows that the efficacy of the sacred waters was appropriated by Christians), there is the possibility the Saxons targeted Buxton for exactly this reason. Taking the Britons' shrine would have struck them a demoralizing blow. If the goddess or saint or goddess-become-saint is herself not safe from the depredations of the barbarians, who is?

A threat to such a shrine may well have galvanized British resistence. Arthur himself may have been called upon to lead the British in the defense of Nemetia's waters and her temple-grove.

The three days and three nights Arthur bore the cross (or, rather, a shield bearing an image of a cross) at Badon in the *Welsh Annals* are markedly similar to the three days and three nights Urien is said to have blockaded the Saxons in the island of Lindsfarne (British Metcaud) in Chapter 63 of the HB. In Gildas, immediately before mention of Badon, we have the following phrase: *"From then on victory went now to our countrymen, now to their enemies..."* Similarly, just prior mention of Urien at Lindisfarne, we have this: *"During that time, sometimes the enemy, sometimes the Cymry were victorious..."* It would seem, therefore, that either the motif of the three days and three nights was taken from the Urien story and inserted into that of Arthur or vice-versa.

What is fascinating about this parallel is that Lindisfarne or *'Holy Island'*, as it came to be known, was an important spiritual centre of Northern Britain. The inclusion of the three days and three nights (an echo of the period Christ spent in the tomb) in the Badon story suggests that we can no longer accept the view that Arthur's portage of Christian symbols at Badon was borrowed solely from the Castle Guinnion battle account in the HB. Aquae Arnemetiae, like Lindisfarne, was a holy place. Arthur's fighting there may have been construed as a holy act.

Supposedly, 960 Saxons were slain by Arthur at Badon. In the past, most authorities have seen in the number 960 no more than a fanciful embellishment on the *Annals'* entry, i.e. more evidence of Arthur as a *'legend in the making'*. But 960 could be a very significant number, militarily speaking. The first cohort of a Roman legion was composed of six doubled centuries or 960 men. As the most important unit, the first cohort guarded the Roman Imperial eagle standard. Now, while the Roman army in the late period no longer possessed a first cohort composed of this number of soldiers, it is possible Nennius's 960 betrays an antiquarian knowledge of earlier Roman military structure. However, why the Saxons are said to have lost such a number cannot be explained in terms of such an anachronistic description of a Roman unit.

The simplest explanation for Nennius's 960 is that it represents 8 Saxon long hundreds, each long hundred being composed of 120 warriors. To quote from Tacitus on the Germanic long hundred:

> "On general survey, their [the German's] strength is seen to lie rather in their infantry, and that is why they combine the two arms in battle. The men who they select from the whole force and station in the van are fleet of foot and fit admirably into cavalry action. The number of these chosen men is exactly fixed. A hundred are drawn from each district, and 'the hundred' is the name they bear at home. What began as a mere number ends as a title of distinction" [Germania 6]

Curiously, in the Norse poem *Grimnismal*, 8 hundreds of warriors (probably 960) pass through each of the doors of Valhall, the Hall of the Slain, at the time of Ragnarok or the Doom of the Powers.

THE THIRTEENTH BATTLE: CAMLANN

After these many victories, Arthur is said to have perished with Medraut at a place called Camlann. Camlann has long been linked with Camboglanna, the *'Crooked Bank'*, a Roman fort towards the western end of Hadrian's Wall. The only other candidates for Camlann are in NW Wales (the Afon Gamlan and two other Camlanns near Dolgellau), and these do not have anything to do with the Northern Arthur.

Crawford pointed out that the best etymology for Camlann would actually be B. *Cambolanda*, *'Crooked Enclosure'*, an utterly unknown name, but Jackson had no problem with the derivation from Camboglanna.

Those who point to Camelon on the Antonine Wall are ignorant of the fact that this place was originally called Carmuirs. It was renamed Camelodunum in 1526 by the antiquarian Hector Boece. However, an inscription found at the Camelon fort (RIB 2210) reads:

CAMELON VEX LEG XX V V F

The problem with interpreting the Camelon in this inscription as the name of the Camelon fort is the presence in the same inscription of Legio XX Valeria Victrix. The Twentieth Legion is well known to have had its first British base at Colchester, whose Roman name was Camulodunum. Doubtless, this inscription merely calls attention to this fact. The Camelon fort has been identified with the Colania of Ptolemy and the *Ravenna Cosmography*.

The Castlesteads fort sits on a high bluff overlooking the Cambeck valley and the break on the mosses to the north-west which carries the modern road from Brampton to Longtown. The site was drastically leveled in 1791, when the gardens of Castlesteads House were laid out and today nothing is visible of the fort aprt from the southern edge of the fort platform, while the view described above is obscured by trees. The Cam Beck has so far eroded the north-west front of the fort that the side gates now lie only 50 ft from the edge of the gorge. From east to west the fort measures 394 ft and it is thought to have been originally about 400 ft square, covering some 3.75 acres, though it is not impossible that the fort faced south rather than north and was therefore somewhat larger.

Excavations in 1934 revealed the east, west and south walls of the fort, the east and west double-portal gates and south-west angle tower. The gate towers were built one course deeper than the fort wall, whose foundations were the normal 6 ft wide. All walls had been heavily robbed, but roof-tiles occurred in a number of the towers at ground-floor level, suggesting the possibility of oven-bases, as at Birdoswald, rather than collapsed roofs. Space allowed only for the identification of one ditch, 16 ft wide. No contact has been made with any internal building, but an external bath-house was located and partly dug in 1741.

Figure 15 - Site of Castlesteads Roman Fort

Castlesteads is unique along the whole Wall for sitting between the Wall and Vallum but not being attached to the former; presumably either its pre-existence or the lie of the land dictated its location.

A carved stone dated roughly 466-599 CE was found at Castlesteads. Because in the past the inscription has been read wrongly, i.e. upside down as *'BEDALTOEDBOS'*, this has been considered a corrupt attempt at the divine name BELATUCADROS, altars to whom were found here in a Roman context. However, the inscription actually reads *'SUB DEO LAUDIB[US]'*, which according to Professor David Howlett of Oxford can be translated as *'with the accompaniment of praises of God'*. Thus this stone clearly denotes a Christian presence at Castlesteads during the time of Arthur.

A Note on the Name Medraut/Modred (= the later Mordred)

On February 26, 1996, I received a letter from Professor Oliver Padel of Cambridge. This was in response to a query I had sent him some time earlier in which I proposed that the name Medrawt – born by the personage who died with Arthur at Camlann – may represent the Roman name Moderatus. What Padel had to say on this possibility is important enough for Arthurian studies to be reprinted in full below:

> "Not much has been done on the name of Medrawt or Mordred... In an article on various words in Welsh with the root med, Medr-, Ifor Williams suggested that the name might be connected with the Welsh verb medru 'to be able, to hit'; but he did not develop the idea, only mentioned it in passing.
>
> Middle Welsh Medrawt cannot formally be identical with Old Cornish Modred, Old Breton Modrot (both of which are recorded, indicating an original Old Co.Br. *Modrod), since the Welsh e in the first syllable should not be equivalent to a Co.Br. o there.
>
> What people do not seem to have asked is what this discrepancy means: we can hardly say that Welsh Medrawt is a different name, since it clearly belongs to the same character as Geoffrey's [Geoffrey of Monmouth] Modredus < Co.Br. Modrod. Which is 'right'? I would suggest that the Co.Br. form is the ancient one, and that the Welsh form has been altered, perhaps indeed by association with the verb medru.
>
> That was already my conclusion, but I did not have a derivation for Modrod. However, Modrod would be the exact derivative of Latin Moderatus, as you suggest. Your suggestion is most attractive, and neither I nor (so far as I know) anyone else has previously thought of it.
>
> Like you, I should be relucatant to say that Modrod couldn't have a Celtic derivation; but it fits so well with Moderatus that I personally don't feel the need to look further."

If Medrawt or, rather, Modrod, is Moderatus, this may be significant for a Medraut at Cambloglanna on Hadrian's Wall, for we know of a Trajanic period prefect named C. Rufius Moderatus, who left inscriptions at Greatchesters on the Wall and Brough-under-Stainmore in Cumbria (CIL iii. 5202, RIB 1737, 166-9, 2411, 147-51). The name of this prefect could have become popular in the region and might even have still been in use among Northern British noble families in the 6th century CE.

It is only later tradition which makes Arthur and Medraut enemies at Camlann. In the *Welsh Annal* entry, we are only told that both chieftains fell at this site.

CONCLUSION: ARTHUR'S MILITARY ROLE IN THE NORTH

I would say that the following battles from the HB and AC should indeed be attributed to Arthur:

- *Mouth of the Glein*
- *Dubglas River in Linnuis*
- *Bassas River*
- *Celidon Wood*
- *Castle Guinnion*
- *City of the Legions*
- *Mount Badon*
- *Camlann*

These battles, however, I consider problematic and perhaps doubtful:

- *Tribruit shore (see above and Chapter 4 below)*
- *Breguoin*
- *Agned (Agued)*

Arthur may simply have been recognized as the strongest war-leader or field general of the time and did exactly what HB 56 said he did: *"fought against them [the Saxons] in those days, together with the kings of the British; but he was their leader in battle."* There is no indication that he was a king like the next generation's Urien of Rheged, although he was not lacking in royal blood and was, in fact, related to Urien. He appears to have made up for this deficiency in military skill and might.

Arthur is only referred to in our earliest sources as *dux bellorum*, 'battle-leader', and *miles*, 'soldier'. This suggests that he acted as a general over the armies of other kings, and may, therefore, have performed a mercenary or federate function. I think that the mercenary notion is unlikely, if he did have the royal connections I have outlined above.

Arthur's father Uther may also have been a soldier and not a king. His epithet Pendragon or Chief-dragon is interesting in this regard. While the epithet is usually interpreted according to later Welsh usage of the word dragon as a poetic term for a warrior, chieftain or hero, Pendragon matches to an uncanny degree an actual Roman army rank known to have existed in the fifth century CE, i.e. the time of Uther's floruit. To quote from Robert Vermaat's *The Draco: The Late Roman Military Standard*:

> "By the fifth century, as may be deduced from inscriptions from Perge and Prusias/Üskübü, Turkey, as well as from a poem by Prudentius, there was a rank called magister draconum. This officer was the superior of the draconarii in a unit, ranking immediately below the tribune. However, we don't know if he directed the draconarii in battle, or may just have been the head of the standard bearers' club or scholae. The magister draconum probably replaced the optio signiferorum, whose function unfortunately is equally vague."

Could Arthur, then, have been the son of a man who held the Roman-derived rank of Magister Draconum? There is nothing far-fetched about this notion, as long as we accept the possibility that some Roman military customs continued to be observed by the British elite in northwestern England a century or so after the withdrawal of the legions.

An alternative would be to see Arthur as being appointed supreme military commander over the region by a council of chieftains. This would be similar to the famous Scotsman William Wallace being made *'Lord Protector'* – although, of course, Wallace was a commoner. In my opinion, Arthur, while most assuredly of royal blood, was a shrewd, strong and popular military leader who was able to unite warring British factions against a common enemy and repeatedly win victories against that enemy on several fronts. His military successor and blood relative Urien benefited from his success.

CHAPTER 4

ARTHUR'S OTHER BATTLES: MYTHOLOGICAL OR MISTAKEN

1) THE PA GUR BATTLE SITES

The Arthur presented to us in the early Welsh poem *Pa Gur* is a very different personage from the one we find in the battle list of Nennius' HB. In *Pa Gur*, Arthur numbers among his men the mythological Manawyd(an) son of Llyr. He and his men fight monsters and witches. We have clearly departed from history and have embraced the realm of the fantastic.

While the *Pa Gur* is, alas, a fragmentary poem, the following battles or locations are listed in the order in which they occur:

- *Tryfrwyd*
- *Din Eidyn*
- *Celli*
- *Afarnach's hall*
- *Dwellings of Dissethach*
- *Din Eidyn*
- *Shore of Tryfrwyd*
- *Upland of Ystawingun*
- *Mon*

I have proposed above that Traeth Tryfrwyd may be Broken Hook near the Avon in what had been Manau Gododdin.

Din Eidyn, as is well known, is Edinburgh. Arthur's opponents in this battle are the Cynbyn or *'Dog-heads'*, whom I believe to be an echo of the Venicones tribe.

Afarnach's hall may be a reference to the Pictish capital of Abernethy. Watson discussed the etymology of Abernethy as follows:

> "Thus *Abur-nethige* of the Pictish Chronicle, now Abernethy near Perth, has as its second part the Genitive of a nominative *Nethech* or *Neitheach (fem.)*, which is Gaelicized either from *Neithon* directly, or from a British river name from the same root."

I would add that Neithon comes from an original Nechtan or Neachtan, which appears to be cognate with L. Neptune.

Abernethy is on the border region between the Pictish kingdoms of Fortriu and Circenn. We have seen above that the Dalriadan Arthur is said to have fought in Circenn, and the Abernethy/Afarnach battle may well be a traditional memory of the Circenn conflict. This would mean that the Irish references to the Dalriadan Arthur being both in the territory of the Miathi and in Circenn were known to Welsh tradition, which then proceeded to place the British Arthur wrongly at Traeth Tryfrwyd in Miathi territory and at Abernethy on the border of Circenn. I have already stated that the British Arthur's *'northern line'* of battles seems properly to have run just south of the Tweed.

If Afarnach is Abernethy, we may presume that Celli, the *'Grove'*, was to be found somewhere in the region that stretched between Edinburgh and Abernethy. Unfortunately, there are many Gaelic grove place-names (*coille* and variants) as well as English place-name elements with similar meanings in this part of central Scotland, so it may well prove impossible to locate the Celli where Cai is said to have fought. As its being lost is emphasized in the poem (*Pan colled kelli*, *'when lost was Celli'*), we must assume it was a place of some importance.

I would very tentatively put forward a connection between Celli, *'Grove'*, and the Medionemeton or *'Middle Sacred Grove'* mentioned in the *Ravenna Cosmography*. The

Ravenna Cosmography situates the Medionemeton between the entries for the *'Camelon'* Roman fort and the Ardoch Roman fort, and this would accord well with a Celli between Edinburgh and Abernethy. To date, two proposed identifications for the nemeton have been offered: Cairnpapple in West Lothian and the Arthur's Oven shrine which once stood near Larbert, a town across the Carron River from Camelon. Arthur's Oven is almost certainly the structure mentioned in the HB of Nennius:

> *Chapter 23: "The Emperor Carausius rebuilt it [the Antonine Wall] later, and fortified it with seven forts, between the two estuaries, and a Round House of polished stone, on the banks of the river Carron..."*

Dissethach, where Arthur's opponent is Pen Palach, looks like Tig Scathach, *'House of Scathach'*, and Beinn na Caillich (allowing for the difference between P- and Q- Celtic), *'Hill of the Witch'*. Dunsgiath or Dun Scathach, the *'Fort of Scathach'*, and Beinn na Caillich, are both in the southeast of the Isle of Skye. From Beatrix Faerber, CELT project manager, we learn that there is a reference in *Tochmarc Emire*, which incorporates the story of Cu Chulainn's training at arms with Scathach. In this case, Scathach's house is *tig Scathgi* (= Schathaigi).

The upland of (Y)stawingun, where nine witches are slain by Cei, is quite possibly Stanton Moor in Derbyshire, where we find the stone circle called the Nine Ladies. The *'lord of Emrys'* mentioned in the poem just prior to (Y)stawingun is a known periphrasis for Gwynedd, as Ambrosius/Emrys was the traditional lord of that land. Emrys in this context may actually be a reference to the Amber river, which lies just east of Stanton Moor.

The *–gun*, if from an earlier *–cun*, could have come about by mistaking in MS. an original t for c. The middle *–w–* may represent a u, such as is found in Staunton, a known variant of Stanton.

Much later story substitutes the hero Peredur and transplants the witches to Gloucester, presumably because of the presence in Gloucestershire of towns named Stanton and Staunton.

FIGURE 16 - NINE LADIES OF STANTON MOOR

There is no mystery regarding Mon, as this is the common Welsh name for the Isle of Anglesey in northwest Wales. Welsh tradition insists that Cath Palug or Cath Palug, which Cai battles on Mon, is the cat of a person called Palug. Modern scholars prefer to view palug as perhaps meaning *'scratching'* or *'clawing'*, hence Cath Palug as the Clawing Cat.

Cath Palug is linked in line 82 of the poem to *'lleuon'*, i.e. lions. The association of lions with Arfon (where the cat is born) and Mon may have to do with the simple confusion of *llew*, *'lion'*, for *lleu*, the god who is the Lord of Gwynedd in Welsh tradition. The letters u and w readily substitute for each other.

2) TWO ADDITIONAL POETIC REFERENCES

Much has been made of early references to Arthur in three important poems: *The Gododdin*, *Marwnad Cynddylan* and *Geraint son of Erbin*. As I have discussed *The Gododdin* reference already above (Chapter 3) in the context of Arthur's battle at Mount Agned, here I will restrict myself to a brief treatment of the other two poems.

Marwnad Cynddylan

Scholar Jenny Rowland has done a very nice job of disposing of the difficulty posed by Line 46 of *Marwnad Cynddylan*. The line in question reads:

Canawon artir wras dinas degyn

This has in the past been amended to read:

Canawon Arthur wras dinas degyn: "whelps of Arthur, a resolute protection"

Jenny Rowland, wisely, opts instead for:

Canawon artir[n]wras dinas degyn, i.e.: Canawon arddyrnfras dinas degyn: "strong-handed whelps..."

This nicely eliminates our having to associate Arthur with the Powys kingdom in east-central Wales.

Geraint son of Erbin

A harder thing to dispose of is the presence of Arthur's name in the poem *Geraint son of Erbin*. While different versions of the poem exist, all are in agreement in including the name Arthur in one of their stanzas. This would not be a problem, were it not for the fact that, in Jenny Rowland's words, *"Despite the Arthurian link in Geoffrey of Monmouth's work there can be no question that 'Geraint fab Erbin' is older than the Historia Regum Britanniae."* In other words, someone, for some reason, seems to have placed Arthur in Dumnonia (Devon and Cornwall) prior to Geoffrey of Monmouth's doing so.

If, as is genuinely agreed, *Geraint son of Erbin* is to be dated between the ninth and eleventh centuries, how do we account for Arthur being in Dumnonia? This is a critical question, for Geraint son of Erbin would seem to be our earliest source seeking to situate Arthur in extreme southwest England.

Using Rowland's composite text, I can make the following observations: Geraint's name occurs in 18 out of 27 stanzas. To these we may add a 19th stanza containing *'the son of Erbin'*. Other than the names of Geraint and Erbin, and the single occurrence of the name of Arthur, there are no other personal names in the poem.

Also, it is suspicious that Arthur's name is used in exactly the same way as is that of Geraint. The variants of the *'Arthurian'* line are as follows:

> *"En Llogporth y gueleise Arthur...*
>
> *En llogporth y gueleise y Arthur...*
>
> *Yn llongborth llas y Arthur..."*

Professor Patrick Sims-Williams has suggested that to solve the problem posed by the *'syntactically and semantically ambiguous'* y before Arthur's name that this line be considered *'a poetic inversion'* for *'men to (i.e. vassals of) Arthur'*, the *'men'* in question being the warriors of the following line:

Gwyr dewr kymynynt a/o dur; "brave men, they hewed with steel"

The *Red Book of Hergest* has instead: "In Llongborth Arthur lost brave men, they hewed with steel"

Of course, the y is in front of Arthur's name even in the *Red Book* version. The odd thing about the poem is that Geraint's name is used in exactly the same context. We have the *Black Book of Carmarthen's*:

En Llogporth y llas y Gereint...

Which is, however, rendered in the *Red Book of Hergest* as

En Llogporth y llas Gereint...

The cumulative effect of the panegyric, with its formulaic repetition of Geraint's name, and the sudden intrusion of Arthur's within the same cymeriad, is designed to enable us to see Arthur in this context not as a separate individual, but as an honorific being applied to Geraint.

In other words, just as we find a warrior in *The Gododdin* compared unfavorably to Arthur, who is there decidedly a famous figure of the past, in the Geraint fab Erbin elegy the heroic nature of Geraint is so great during the Llongporth battle that he symbolically **is** Arthur, the *'emperor'* and *'ruler of battle'*.

Those who attempt to account for Arthur's presence in the poem have in the past resorted to two explanations. First, that Arthur really was there, which would put this particular Geraint back in Arthur's time, or that a warrior troop whose predecessors had served under Arthur was still, in Geraint's day, referred to as *'Arthur's men'*.

There are two problems with these explanations. In the first case, it seems fairly certain that the Llongporth battle is to be identified with the battle fought at Langport by the Wessex chieftains Ine and Nunna against a Dumnonian Geraint in c. 710. This event is memorialized in the ASC, where it is described as a Saxon victory. Needless to say, the 8th century is well outside the time period of Arthur.

That the men fighting with Geraint are composed of a troop whose members originally flocked to Arthur's standard makes little sense, given that the same *'brave men'* (*gwyr dewr*) are ascribed to Geraint:

> *"In Llongborth Geraint lost [or 'I saw to']*
>
> *Brave men from the region of Dyfnaint.*
>
> *And before they were killed, they killed."*

In following Geraint, these warriors were fighting for a chieftain who in the praise language of the poem was an incarnation of Arthur. While it could be argued that Geraint's fighting alongside Arthur or the latter's men might be considered praise enough, from the perspective of the panegyrist, whose sole goal was to glorify Geraint, to use Arthur or his men in this fashion would actually have diminished Geraint's stature. Why would a poet seeking to praise Geraint distract his audience by calling attention to the presence of another, greater hero?

We need only ask this final question: who is greater, a Geraint who by virtue of his martial prowess is literally an Arthur, or a Geraint who needs the help of Arthur and/or Arthur's men in battle?

3) THE THREE PRISONS OF ARTHUR

Triad 52 of the *Triads of the Island of Britain* concerns itself with the *'Three Exalted Prisoners of the Island of Britain'*. After listing the three prisoners, the Triad continues as follows:

> *"And one [prisoner], who was more exalted than the three of them, was three nights in prison in Caer Oeth and Anoeth, and three nights imprisoned by Gwen Pendragon, and three nights in an enchanted prison under the stone of Echymeint [Llech Echemeint]. This exalted prisoner was Arthur."*

Can we identify these prisons and Gwen Pendragon with known places or personages? Might they have had something to do with the Arthurian battle sites?

Gwen Pendragon has not been identified in the past. Gwen is the feminine form of Gwyn and means *'the white or fair one'* (later, the *'blessed one'*). It is possible that here Gwen is being used as an eponym for the Guinnion of Castellum Guinnion, an Arthurian battle site in Nennius. However, given that one of the famous dragons of Dinas Emrys was white we should perhaps interpret Gwen as the genius of the Saxons. This white dragon was found by Emrys (or Ambrosius, later identified wrongly by Geoffrey of Monmouth with Myrddin/Merlin) in a subterranean context. This monster's companion in the *'Otherworld'* below Dinas Emrys was the red dragon, the genius of the British people. It is my guess that here Arthur is being identified with the red dragon, buried in the prison of the white *'chief dragon'*, a comparable leader of the Saxons.

According to Geoffrey of Monmouth, both Ambrosius, uncle of Arthur, and Uther, Arthur's father, were buried at Stonehenge next to Amesbury, ancient Ambresbyrig, a site confused in the tradition with Dinas Emrys. Arthur placed in a typical *'death-prison'* at Stonehenge with his father and uncle may preserve an otherwise lost Welsh tradition which runs counter to the more popular one situating him at Avalon on the western end of Hadrian's Wall in Cumbria.

FIGURE 17 - DINAS EMRYS

The Llech or Stone of Echemeint would appear to be a reference to Bath, which the Welsh identified with Arthur's Mount Badon. According to the ASC (year entry 973 CE), Bath was also known by the name Acemannes-ceaster. This alternate name for Bath appears to be a development from the ancient Romano-British names for the town, Aquae Sulis and Aquae Calidae

And what about Caer Oeth and Anoeth? Oeth means *'something difficult to obtain or achieve, a difficulty, a wonder; something strange or wonderful'*. Anoeth has essentially the same meaning, as the prefix *an-* is merely an intensifier: *'a wonder, something difficult to acquire; something strange or difficult'*. The *Stanzas of the Graves* used anoeth, where it is said of Arthur that his final resting place in this world is a *'wonder'* (*"anoeth bid bet y Arthur"*). The implied sense may be that his grave was considered *'difficult'* to locate, precisely because its location was a mystery. Or, perhaps, the grave was imposible to find because it was in Avalon and Avalon was manifestly an Otherworld.

The Caer Oeth and Anoeth placename is also mentioned in the *Mabinogion* tale *Culhwch and Olwen*, where it is one of the castles Arthur boasts of gaining entrance to. Once again, in the *Stanzas of the Graves* we are told that the burial ground of the host of Caer Oeth and Anoeth can be found in Gwanas, a mountain tract located near Cadair Idris in Ceredigion.

In my opinion, the word anoeth holds the key to identifying this prison's location. It surely must represent the Agned or Agued (*'dire straits, great difficulty, anxiety, distress'*) of Nennius and Geoffrey of Monmouth, which is found in the *Brut y Brenhinedd* (the Welsh version of Geoffrey's *History*) as Mynydd Agned. Oddly enough, we do not find Agned in the early Welsh literature outside of the *Brut*. Instead, Arthur is placed at Din Eidyn or Edinburgh (see *The Black Book of Carmarthen's* poem *'Who is the Porter?'*), which as the Castle of Maidens and the Dolorous Mountain was identified by Geoffrey of Monmouth with Mount Agned. The Caer *'Anoeth'* of Arthur may well be a relic of Arthur's Agned.

Rachel Bromwich, in her notes to the translation of Triad 52, states that *"Caer Oeth and Anoeth may be an old title which, like similar phrases... has become so corrupted in transmission that its original constituents are no longer recognizable."* As the word *agwed* is a very rare one, and does not appear in later texts, it is quite conceivable that *anoeth* was substituted for it, at least in the context of the Arthurian battle name.

CHAPTER 5

THE NORTHERN KINGDOMS

To give some idea of the political landscape of Arthur's Northern Britain, it might be helpful to investigate the Northern princes and the kingdoms they controlled.

The most northern of these kingdoms was, of course, the ancient territory of the Votadini or Gododdin, which in the Roman period is believed to have stretched from the Wear or the Tyne through Northumberland and the Lothians to the Forth.

The term *'Lothian'* appears to have been of Dark Age origin, which as we have seen stands for an original Lleudiniawn, *'Place of the Fort of [the god] Lugus'*. There is an eponymous king recorded in the *Life of St. Kentigern* called Leudonus, i.e. Lleuddun, and his kingdom in Welsh was known as Lleuddunion. He was supposed to have ruled from Traprain Law, which was earlier called Dunpelder, the *'Fort of the Spear (shaft)'*.

In the late 6th century, the king of the Votadini was, apparently, one Mynyddog Mwynfawr. He is said to have ruled from Din Eidyn or Edinburgh and was the son of a certain Ysgyran, and probably succeeded Clydno Eidyn. *The Gododdin* poem implies that the Britons who fought the English at Cattraeth assembled at Mynyddog's court at Edinburgh. Clydno Eidyn, in turn, was the son of Cynfelyn son of Dyfnwal Hen. Myynyddog is also given the epithet *'Eidyn'* meaning, undoubtedly, *'of Eithne'*. Once again, Eidyn is likely the British form of Eithne, mother of the god Lugh in Irish tradition.

Pabo Post Prydain, the *'Pillar of Britain'*, is the son of Ceneu son of Coel Hen, both famous chieftains of the North. Pabo is spelled Pappo in the genealogies appended to the HB.

Coel Hen's name is believed to be preserved in Kyle in Ayreshire.

A son of Pabo is Dunod Fwr, who is probably the chieftain who fought against the Rheged princes in Erechwydd, which itself is usually placed somewhere in Cumbria. We may relate this Dunod to Dent in NorthWest Yorkshire, his lands here being termed the *'regio Dunotinga'*, kingdom of the descendents of Dunod. From John Morris's *The Age of Arthur*:

> "DENT: regio Dunotinga is one of four districts of north-western Yorkshire overrun by the English in or before the 670s, Eddius 17 [Life of Wilfrid]. The passage is overlooked in EPNS WRY 6, 252, where the early spellings Denet(h) are rightly related to a British Dinned or the like, and Ekwall's derivation from a non-existent British equivalent of the Old Irish dind, hill, is properly dismissed. EPNS does not observe that Dent was, and still is, the name of a considerable region, and tha thte village is still locally known as Dent Town, in contrast with the surrounding district of Dent.... Regio Dunotinga plainly takes its name from a person named Dunawt, Latin Donatus, as does the district of Dunoding in Merioneth, named from another Dunawt, son of Cunedda."

The regio Dunotinga was associated with the Ribble and other places in the north of the West Riding. As the Dent River is a tributary of the upper Lune in Lonsdale, and Upper Lonsdale seems to have been within the canton of the ancient Carvetii tribe, it is likely that Dunot was himself descended from the *'People of the Stag'*. The Carvetii ruled over what we now think of as Cumbria and adjacent areas.

Another son of Pabo's is Cerwyd or Cerwydd, who is otherwise completely unknown. This name is transparently an eponym for the Carvetii tribe. We have just seen that Dunod's Dent seems to have been a part of the territory once covered by this ancient tribal kingdom.

The form Cerwydd as a direct eponym for the Carvetii is not possible; we would need Cerwyd for an exact linguistic correspondence. However, as Cerwydd means *'stag-like one'*, we can say with a fair degree of certainty that he does represent the People of the Stag.

As for Pabo, father of Dunod, we may situate him at Papcastle (Pabecastr in 1260), the Derventio Roman fort in Cumbria. *Pap-* is thought to be from ON *papa, papi,* for *'hermit',* but this seems an unlikely name for a *'ceaster'.* Instead we should look to early W. *pab, 'pope',* i.e. *papa,* pl. *pabeu,* and Llanbabo church of St. Pabo in Anglesey. Pabo's Chester would seem to do quite nicely. We could then locate Pabo within the Carvetii kingdom of his sons Cerwyd/Cerwydd and Dunod.

I would add that Pabo's epithet *'Post'* or *'Pillar'* is possibly a reference to the Solway, which is believed to be from OScand. *sul, 'pillar or post',* and *vath, 'ford'.* It has been proposed, quite reasonably I think, that the pillar or post of the Solway is the Lochmaben Stone at Gretna Green. A *'papa'* or *'father'* of the post/pillar named for the Divine Son Mabon makes for an interesting combination of place-name elements!

Sawyl Benisel ("Low-head"), yet another son of Pabo, is dated c. 480 CE. On the Ribble, not far south of *'regio Dunotinga',* is a town called Samlesbury. The place-name expert Eilert Ekwall has Samlesbury as *'Etymology obscure',* but then proposes OE sceamol, *'bench',* as its first element, possibly in the topographical sense of *'ledge'.* A.D. Mills follows Ekwall by saying that this place-name is probably derived from *scamol* plus *burh* (dative *byrig*). However, *sceamol/scamol* is not found in other place-names where a *'ledge'* is being designated. Instead, the word *scelf/scielf/scylfe, 'shelf of level or gently sloping ground, ledge'* is used.

I would suggest as a better etymology for Samlesbury: *'Sawyl's fort'.* There are, for example, Sawyl place-names in Wales (Llansawel, Pistyll Sawyl, now Ffynnon Sawyl). Sawyl is the Welsh form of the name Samuel.

Dr. Andrew Breeze of Pamplona, a noted expert on British place-names, agrees with this proposed etymology:

"I feel sure you are right. The form surely contains the Cumbric equivalent of Welsh _Sawyl_<_Samuel_. Your explanation of this toponym in north Lancashire is thus new evidence for Celtic survival in Anglo-Saxon times."

Now that we have placed Pabo and his descendents on the map, we need to investigate what has been explained as an intrusion on their pedigree.

An Arthwys and his father Mar are both inserted into the Pabo genealogy. Instead of Pabo son of Ceneu son of Coel Hen, we have Pabo sone of Arthwys son of Mar son of Ceneu, etc. This same Arthwys is made the grandfather of a Cynwyd of the tribal group known as the Cynwydion (of the Kent river in Cumbria - Kent being from Kennet, which in Welsh is Cynwyd), of Gwenddolau of Carwinley (Caer Gwenddolau just a little north of Carlisle/Stanwix) and father of Eliffer (Eleutherius) of York. Eliffer in another pedigree is the son of Gwrgwst Ledlum (Fergus Mor of Dalriada) son of Ceneu son of Coel Hen.

Mar is made the father of Lleenog, father of Gwallog of the kingdom of Elmet (a small kingdom centreed about Leeds, probably from Welsh *elfydd*, *'world, land'*), but in another pedigree it is Maeswig Gloff, i.e. Maeswig *'the Lame'*, who is father of Lleenog.

Mar, whose name is also written Mor, as an intrusion in the Pabo genealogy, would seem to represent the Moringas of Westmorland. According to Ekwall, Westmorland or Westmoringaland, the *'Land of the West Moringas'*, is a people of the Yorkshire Moors (from OE *mor*). Mills adds that this territorial designation alludes *'to the North Yorkshire Pennines'*. As this region was adjacent to Elmet, Mar was made the father of Lleenog, father of Gwallog of Elmet.

If Mar/Mor is an eponym for Westmorland, and he boasts descendents who ruled the kingdom of Elmet, and his son Arthwys could claim descendents who ruled at Carwinley near Liddesdale just to the northwest of Carlisle, in the Kent valley of southern Cumbria and, possibly, at York, then it is understandable that his family connections and those belonging to other rulers of the region would become intertwined.

Maeswig Gloff (Masguic Clop in the Harleian genealogies) was, presumably, a ruler of Westmorland. His name could be from *Magos-vicos, 'Fighter of the Plain'. However, I should not neglect to point out that the Roman fort at Burrow Walls, Workington, Cumbria, was named Magis, formed from British *magos, 'plain'. Papcastle of Pabo is on the Derwent only a few miles east of Magis, itself at the mouth of the same river.

The name Arthwys has frequently been brought into connection with that of Arthur. Unfortunately, this name is from Arth-, 'Bear', + –(g)wys, which in the early period was comparable to Irish fios, 'knowledge'. Hence he was the 'Bear of Knowledge' or, perhaps, 'Bear-knowing'. As I showed in my book The Secrets of Avalon, the etymology of Arthur is from the Roman Artorius.

FIGURE 18 - ARTHURET KNOWES

Not far west of the Carwinley of Gwenddolau on the coast of Galloway is the fort of Caerlaverock. The name of this fort is referred to in Welsh tradition as the 'Lark's Nest' and it is said to have been the cause of the Battle of Arfderydd

(Arthuret). But *'lark'* is itself either a mistake or pun for the personal name Llywarch, in this case Llywarch Hen son of Elidir Lydanwyn. Llywarch was first cousin to Urien Rheged. Caerlaverock is, therefore, Caer Llywarch.

There is another interesting reference to a place in Cumbria that I might mention. In the *'Cambridge'* group of HB MSS., an interpolation tells us that Vortigern is said to have built *'Guasmoric near Carlisle, a city which in English is called Palme castre.'* While Palme castre has been firmly identified with the Old Carlisle Roman fort one mile south of Wigton in the parish of Westward, this is clearly a misidentification on the part of the interpolator.

As has been suggested before, Guasmoric must be Gwas Meurig, the *'Abode of Meurig or Mauricius'*. This is clearly an attempt at rendering the Gabrosentum Roman fort in Cumbria at Moresby. According to the place-name authorities, Moresby (Moriceby, Moresceby) is Maurice's By, Maurice being a Norman name and *-by* being OScand for *'farmstead, village, settlement'*. Whether we can propose an original Welsh Meurig underlying Maurice is questionable. In all likelihood, the interpolation is late and Guasmoric represents Maurice's By. If originally a Meurig place-name, this may commemorate the 6th century Meurig son of Idno son of Meirchion, who married a daughter of Gwallog of Elmet.

As archaeology has shown us, there were two main centres for the Carvetii kingdom. One was the ancient tribal centre near Brougham, the Roman Brocavum, with its triple sacred henges at Eamont. One of these henges is actually called King Arthur's Round Table and another the Little Round Table. There is evidence in the form of a concentration of inscriptions at Brougham that the primary Carvetii deity worshipped at these henges was a horned god (doubtless a stag, given that Carvetii means *'People of the Stag'*) named Belatucadros.

The other power centre, Carlisle/Stanwix, I will discuss below (see Chapter 6).

But there was also an important region called variously Erechwydd or Yr Echwydd, mentioned in connection with

Urien, his sons, Gwallog son of Lleenog of Elmet and with Dunod Fwr. No wholly satisfactory identification of Erechwydd has yet been made, but it would seem to be somewhere in or close to Cumbria.

What we do know about Erechwydd is that the *Er-* prefix is not the definite article *yr*, even though the name is sometimes wrongly written '*yr echwyd*' in the poetry, but a form of *Ar-*, as found in other place-names, e.g. Arfon. *Ar-* as a prefix originally meant '*in front of*'. But it came to have the senses of '*upon, on, over, at, in, across from*'.

The *National Dictionary of Wales* defines *echwydd* as '*fresh (of water, as opp. to salt); fresh water*'. However, although this meaning has been extrapolated from the contexts in which the word is used, no good etymology had yet been proposed.

I asked Graham Isaac if the word could come from *ech*, '*out of, from*', plus a form of the Indo-European root **ued*, '*wet*'. His response was:

> "The etymology echwydd < *exs-wed-yo-*, or **exs-ud-yo-* (either would probably do it) seems plausible enough."

The literal meaning would then be the '*out-water*', but the sense of the word would be simply '*flowing, fresh water*'. Again, the Welsh texts which use this word leave no doubt that we are talking about fresh water emerging from springs or lakes.

So where was Erechwydd/Yr Echewydd, the '*Place by the flowing, fresh water*'? Our clue lies not only in the name of the region, but in the battles fought there between Dunod Fwr of the Dent region and Gwallog of Elmet against Urien's sons. These engagements are recounted in the *Llywarch Hen* poetry. Given that Urien Rheged seems to have had his origin in Galloway (where we find Dun Ragit, the '*Hill-fort of Rheged*'), and both Dunod and Gwallog had kingdoms in southeastern Cumbria and just southeast of Cumbria, respectively, the most logical place to seek Erechwydd would be the twin valleys of the Eden and Petteril.

A Roman road led from the south up through the valley of the river Lune right past Dunod's Dentdale. This road continued north to the Eden Valley. Another Roman road led west from Leeds and joined with the Lonsdale road. Gwallog could have taken this route to the Eden or he could have gone north up Dere Street and then cut over through the Pennines at Stainmore.

The Eden and Petteril Valleys were the heartland of the ancient Carvetii kingdom. Not only did the twin valleys provide the obvious natural route from Carlisle towards Lancaster and York, the area has been shown to have supported a widespread and occasionally dense pattern of rural settlement in the Roman period.

It is even possible that Erechwydd as a regional designation can be more precisely localized within the Eden and Petteril Valleys. The headwaters of the Petteril lie just WestNorthWest of Eamont. We have already discussed the importance of Eamont with its sacred henges. The river Eamont (a back-formation from the name Eamont itself, from AS *ea-gemot*, '*river-meet*', i.e. confluence) and Lowther join at Eamont Bridge and continue for a short distance eastward to the Eden. There was also, of course, a nexus of Roman roads at Eamont.

In my opinion, the Anglo-Saxon place-name ea-gemot/Eamont may overlie an original British Echwydd. Ekwall thought Eamont refers to the confluence of the Eamont and the stream from Dacre, although given the location of the Brougham/Brocavum Roman fort at the juncture of the Eamont and Lowther, it makes much more sense to see this ea-gemot as the confluence of the latter two rivers. If I am right, then Arechwydd was the Eamont area, specifically the land at and around the Brougham fort and the three Carvetii henges. The '*out-water*' would be a reference specifically to the Eamont, which is formed by the outflow from the Ullswater, the second largest lake in Cumbria.

Just a few miles SouthSouthEast of Eamont is the Lyvennet Beck, a tributary of the Eden. This has been identified with the Llwyfenyd over which Urien is said to have been *'ruler'* (Welsh *teithiawc*).

A NOTE ON GODEU OF THE NORTH AND URBS GIUDI

A very important region in the North of Britain was called Godeu. This place is mentioned in two of the Taliesin praise-poems of Urien. In both cases, Godeu is paired with Reget, i.e. Rheged. Yet Godeu has remained unidentified.

Locating Godeu is complicated by its use in an ancient battle poem called *Kat Godeu*, the *'Battle of Godeu'*. Because this battle poem tells of the god Gwydion's magical activation of an army of trees, it has in the past been assumed that Godeu meant *'forest'*, cf. Welsh *coed/goed*. However, the word *godeu* or *goddeu/goddau* actually existed in early Welsh. The *National Dictionary of Wales* has as the meaning of this word *'intention, design, purpose, object or aim, end in view.'*

There are some clues about where we might find the Godeu of *Kat Godeu*. Firstly, we know Gwydion was most firmly associated with Gwynedd. One other character mentioned in the poem – a certain Peblig, can be put in Gwynedd. The only Peblig known to Welsh tradition was the saint of Llanbeblig, the parish church of Carnarvon. This Peblig is involved in the actual battle in Godeu, at a fort called Caer Nefenhir.

In the *Mabinogion* tale *Math Son of Mathonwy*, Gwydion fights Pryderi of Dyfed in Gwynedd. The battle was fought over some magical swine Gwydion had stolen from Pryderi. Pryderi had gotten these swine from Arawn, king of Annwm, the Welsh Otherworld.

A 17th century account of the *Battle of Godeu* tells us that Amaethon son of Don, Gwydion's brother, had stolen a white roebuck and a whelp from Annwm. The battle was between Arawn and Amaethon. On one side was Bran, a god regularly associated with Gwynedd. In another Taliesin poem, we are told that Lleu also took part in the battle. He, too, was a figure frequently placed in northwestern Wales.

All the clues seem, therefore, to point to Gwynedd as the location of Godeu and Caer Nefenhir.

The fort in question looks to me to be Caer Nefyn Hir, the Fort of Nefyn the Tall (cf. Cai Hir, *'Caius the Tall'*). This points strongly to Nefyn on the Lleyn Peninsula, not far from Peblig's Carnarvon. There are two forts at Nefyn.

The first is the hill-fort of Garn Boduan or Bodfuan, the *'Cairn of the Dwelling of Buan'*. Buan was a saint in the area. The second fort at Nefyn is the promontory fort of Dinllaen, the *'Fort of the Laigin'* or Leinsterman.

But if Nefyn is the location of Caer Nefyn Hir, where is Godeu?

The secret, I believe, lies in the meaning of Godeu – a meaning which will allow us to have not only one Godeu- that which was in or of Gwynedd – but two Godeus, including Urien's region of that name in the North.

The Gododdin kingdom of the North, later called Lothian, derives from a tribal name Votadini. The latter is found in early Welsh documents as Guotodin. Votadini is believed to derive from a personal name or word cognate with Irish Fothad. In Old Irish, *Fothad* or *fothad* means *'basis (?), foundation, founding, support'*. But Irish *fothad* itself is from a root *fotha*, which has among its meanings *'basis'*, *'cause'*, *'charge'*, *'foundation'*, *'reason'*.

I would, therefore, propose that early Welsh Godeu or godeu represents a cognate to Irish fotha and that, as such, it is effectively an abbreviation for Gododdin. Other abbreviations are found for places in the early sources. One example is the *'Aloo'* used in the St. Patrick letters to Ceredig of Strathclyde. *'Aloo'* here represents the first component of Alclud, the *'Rock'* of Clyde.

But if Godeu = Gododdin, what is a Godeu doing on the Lleyn Peninsula in Gwynedd?

The answer to that question is simple: according to the earliest Welsh authority (Nennius in his HB), the founders of Gwynedd, led by the great Cunedda, came down from Manau Gododdin. By calling Gwynedd *'Godeu'*, then, the poets were ackowledging that Gododdin warriors had supposedly established a kingdom in northwest Wales.

Urien's Godeu is Gododdin in the North. The Godeu of Kat Godeu is Gwynedd.

And this brings up a related and important point: the true etymology and location of the Venerable Bede's urbs Giudi on the Firth of Forth. Giudi is found in the epic Welsh poem *The Gododdin* as Iodeo. The 9th century HB spells the place-name Iudeu. Finally, the Middle Irish *Mothers of the Saints* mentions muir n-Giudan, where muir is 'sea', a reference to the Firth of Forth.

It has become customary, for no really good reason, to identify Giudi or Iodeo with Stirling Rock. And this despite the fact that Stirling, anciently Striveling, has a very good and ancient Celtic name. We may compare Striveling with the Welsh place-name Strevelyn or Streflyn (and variants) in Merionethshire. Strevelyn is also known as Llystreflyn or Llystrevelyn, which means the former is probably a contraction for either Llys tref y llyn, *'Court of the settlement of the pool'*, or *Llys tref elin 'Court of the (river-) elbow/bend settlement'*.

Andrew Breeze likens the root of Giudi to Old Welsh *iud*, Middle Welsh *udd*, *'lord'*, and thus interprets the name as meaning *'lord's place, place possessed by a lord'*. As a purely formal etymology, this is quite acceptable.

However, as Breeze himself notes, G- has *'the sound of y in English yes.'* This being so, we can take *The Gododdin* form Iodeo and suppose that this name entered the poem via an English source. In other words, the spelling was originally Godeo or, rather, *'Godeu'*. Thus we can be fairly certain that Bede's Giudi is also Godeu. The urbs Giudi would be the *'city of the Gododdin'*.

Now Bede says that urbs Giudi is *'in medio'* of the Firth of Forth. This does not mean, of course, that the city is in the middle of the Firth, but rather that is it situated in the middle of the shore of the Firth in the Gododdin region. This geographical fix immediately eliminates the traditional Stirling from consideration. However, Din Eidyn, the Dark Age capital of the Gododdin, is itself in the middle portion of the shore of the Firth. I suspect the *'city of the Gododdin'* is, in fact, Din Eidyn. We need not look for urbs Giudi at Stirling or at any of the other places it has been sought (Cramond, Inveresk, etc.).

CHAPTER 6

THE POWER CENTRES OF ARTHUR

1) CAMELOT

The case has often been made that Camelot is a late French form of the Romano-British Camulodunum place-name. However, archaeological evidence from both the fort on Old Lindley Moor near Slack and from the fort on Almondbury five miles from Slack (either of which may have been the ancient Camulodunum) has not revealed Dark Age occupation of these sites. The other primary candidate for Camelot is the Cadbury hill-fort by the Camel villages in Somerset. While this fort does show Dark Age occupation, its location does not match that provided for Camelot in the romances.

The first clue as to the actual whereabouts of Camelot is found in Chretien de Troyes' *Knight of the Cart*, which is the earliest romance to mention this site. According to Chretien, Camelot is *'in the region near Caerleon'*. For some reason, most authorities have seen fit to ignore this statement, insisting that Camelot was placed near Caerleon simply because of Geoffrey of Monmouth's glorified description of the latter site as a major Arthurian centre. If we do take Chretien's statement seriously, we can for the first time arrive at a satisfactory identification of this most magical of royal cities.

The second clue to the location of Camelot is from the later romance *The Quest for the Holy Grail*, wherein Arthur escorts the Grail questers from Camelot to a point just shy of Castle Vagan. A third clue, from the prose *Tristan*, places Camelot either on or very near the sea. The last clue is from the *Morte Artu*; in this source, the castle of Camelot is on a river.

Castle Vagan is St. Fagan's Castle (W. *Ffagan*) four or five miles west of Cardiff. This site lies in the Ely Valley, the supposed location of the Campus Elleti of the boy Ambrosius (not the historical Ambrosius in this context, who was made by Geoffrey of Monmouth into Arthur's uncle, but the *'Divine or Immortal'* Lleu/Mabon; see Chapter 1 above). According to the HB, Campus Elleti, the *'Field or Plain of Elleti'*, was said to be in Glywysing, the later Morgannwg/Glamorgan, which is indeed where the Ely Valley lies. Only a dozen miles separate Campus Elleti from Geoffrey of Monmouth's Caerleon.

The ancient Welsh poem *Pa Gur* tells us of three wizards, one of whom is Mabon, who are styled the *'vultures of Elei'*. This is almost certainly a reference to the Ely River.

In my opinion, Campus Elleti, with Latin Campus rendered as French Champ (the p of which is silent), became Camelot:

Cham(p) ellet(i) > Camelot

So can we now be relatively certain that Camelot was a site in the Ely Valley?

Not really – and for two reasons. First, the Ely has only two significant sites, a Roman villa and the Iron Age hillfort of Caerau. Neither was occupied in the Dark Ages.

Second, there is a major linguistic problem in equating the early forms of the river name Ely with Elleti. And, in fact, it can be demonstrated that the two names cannot originally have designated the same place, something which strongly suggests that Campus Elleti as situated in the Ely Valley is a relocation of another site. This other site would, obviously, have to be a place where Mabon worship is attested.

According to Welsh place-name expert Professor Wyn Owen, the derivation of the Ely river-name is uncertain:

> "R.J. Thomas (Enwau Afonydd a Nentydd Cymru,[Cardiff 1938] 141) derives 'Elei, Istrat Elei' c.1150 tentatively from *Eleg' + -i but offers no meaning, while Ifor Williams (Enawau Lleoedd

[Liverpool 1945] 40) suggests that the root is leg-
meaning dripping, slow-moving from which we get
llaith 'damp', cognate with Eng. to leak, and lake".

The initial E- of Elei could be explained by an *el-* prefix,
'much', would would give us a meaning the *'very slow-*
moving' river. Elleti would have to be, therefore, a form of
Elei which displays the terminal of llaith. Yet if so, it is
difficult to account for why there is only one l in Elei.

Graham Isaac disagrees the the river-name Ely can be
related to Elleti:

> *"On Elei, it would be from the same root as Aled, Alun,*
> *Eleri, all rivers, < Celt. *al- < PIE *h2el-, 'to shine'. They*
> *are all, in different ways, 'shining rivers'. Elleti is not*
> *connected with these. The form Elleti is corroborated by*
> *the instance of 'palude [Latin for "marsh" or "swamp"]*
> *Elleti' in Book of Llan Dav (148). But since both that*
> *and HB's campum Elleti are in Latin contexts, we*
> *cannot see whether the name is OW Elleti (= Elledi) or*
> *OW Ellet (= Elled) with a Latin genitive ending. Both are*
> *possible. My guess would be that OW Elleti is right. As*
> *the W suffix -i would motivate affection, so allowing the*
> *base to be posited as all-, the same as in W ar-all*
> *'other', all-tud 'exile', Gaulish allo-, etc. Elleti would be*
> *'other-place, place of the other side (of something)'.*
> *There are certainly no grounds for thinking of a*
> *connection between Elleti and Elei."*

We are fortunate in that the place-name Elleti may be
found in the form of a personal name at the Corbridge
Roman fort on Hadrian's Wall. It will be recalled that
Arthur's Dubglas River, where several battles were fought, is
the Devil's Water at Linnels very close to Corbridge.

A fragment of a large grey urn was found at Corbridge
bearing the name *ALLIITIO*. This could be the potter's name,
perhaps a form of the nomen Alletius, or the name of the god
portrayed on the fragment. A case has been made for the god
in question being a divine smith, primarily due to the
presence on the urn fragment of what appears to be an anvil
in relief, although there were also metal workings in the
neighborhood of Corbridge. Celtic religion specialist Anne
Ross associates the name Allitio with the same *all-*, *'other'*,
root Isaac links to Elleti. She thinks Allitio may have been a

warrior/smith-god and very tentatively offers *'God of the Otherworld'* for this theonym. I have checked with Isaac and he confirms that this divine name *"would be connected with the Welsh all- I mentioned before."*

FIGURE 19 - CORBRIDGE ROMAN FORT

The name *ALLIITIO* actually occurs twice on one piece of pottery showing feet and a base. This is always assumed to be the base of an anvil, with the feet being those of a smith god. There are a number of sherds of grey pottery from Corbridge with very distinctive applied decoration, with two recognisable themes, the smith god shown with hammer and anvil, and a wheel god who is shown with wheel and club. The fact that the wheel god is depicted by a mould suggests that this type of pottery was being made at Corbridge, though it appears on a number of other sites. The reading occurs twice on this piece of pottery, once in the frame created by the anvil base, and then on the pot below the feet of the standing figure. Another sherd showing the smith god does not have any inscription. John Dore and Stephen

Johnson, who did the captions for the Corbridge Museum gallery, have assumed that the name might be that of a potter, though the Roman Inscriptions of Britrain seems to go for either god or potter.

Astonishingly, of the six inscriptions for Maponus/Mabon in Roman Britain, three belong to Corbridge. These inscriptions are in the form of dedicatory altars, something not found elsewhere in Britain for Maponus.

I would propose that the Campus Elleti of Emrys/Mabon in the HB is a relocation of an Allitio site at Corbridge. The Elei of Mabon, which derives from the root *al-, 'to shine', represents the actual name of the Ely River, to which the northern Campus or Palude Elleti was transferred during the usual development of myth and legend.

While a construction 'Campus Allitio' may be doubted, we can point to the Heaven-field of Bede, said to be close to Hexham, and thus quite possibly near Corbridge. Bede has this as Hefenfelth or 'caelistis campus'. The name is unlikely to be of Christain origin. Instead, we should look to the Roman period dedication (RIB 1131) at Corbridge to Caelistis Brigantia, the 'Heavenly Brigantia'. Caelistis campus would then be a field sacred to the pagan goddess of the Brigantes. In this light, a field sacred to Allitios at or near Corbridge is more plausible.

The Corbridge Roman fort lies on Dere Street at its junction with the Stanegate. The complex of sites stretches from the western outskirts of the modern village of Corbridge for nearly 1 mile westwards along the river terrace. It includes a fort, town, military base, bath-house, mausoleum and bridge. Excavations have demonstrated the existence of five super-imposed forts. The first was not erected earlier than 85 CE. On the basis of the existence in Hexham Abbey of the late-first-century tombstone of Flavinus, a standard bearer of the Ala Petriana, it has been argued that this regiment was the first occupant of the new fort, but this is uncertain. Indeed, there is some evidence to suggest that the fort was larger than even a cavalry regiment would require, as it may have covered at least 13 acres. After some modifications, this fort was dismantled and burnt. A coin of

103 CE found under the east rampart is the only dating evidence for its successor. The new fort may have covered 7 acres and, like its successors, faced south towards the bridge over the Tyne. It was built of turf and timber and, remarkably, the timbers of the headquarters building's shrine are preserved as voids in its stone successor. A change in unit brought changes to this fort. Although the defences and the headquarters remained standing, all other buildings were demolished and replaced. This event is generally associated with the building of Hadrain's Wall. The abandonment of Hadrian's Wall signaled another change. Rebuilding is dated by two inscriptions to the governorship of Lollius Urbicus (139-42 CE) and specifically 139/40 CE and shortly after. The main buildings were now either of stone, or timber placed on stone sill walls, while the barracks-blocks were of timber. Much of the visible, but fragmentary, headquarters building is of this fort. In a subsequent modification, the defences and most principal buildings were retained, but the barracks-blocks were demolished and replaced in stone. To the east of the headquarters a stone building was erected; it is generally interpreted as the commanding officer's house. These changes have been related to the withdrawal from the Antonine Wall and its attendant forts in about 160 CE. Considerable doubt surrounds the date of abandonment of the last fort and the construction of subsequent structures on its site; the later history of Corbridge is obscure. The military installations appear to have continued in use into the late fourth century, and coinage shows that life continued at least in the centre of the town into the period 388-402 CE. At an unknown date the temples were totally demolished and their area given over to kilns, hearths and furnaces; in short, all kinds of industrial activity. The end of the site is also uncertain, although a sufficient number of Anglo-Saxon objects, including a pair of late fifth- or early sixth-century brooches, have been recovered to suggest that a pagan Saxon cemetery existed somewhere within the central area of the Roman town.

2) ETTERBY AS ARTHUR'S BURG

Etterby, in the parish of Stanwix near Carlisle, was called Arthur's burg, according to Joseph Nicolson and Richard Burn's *History and Antiquities of the County of Westmorland and Cumberland, Vol. 2*:

> *"Etterby in old writings is called Arthuriburgum, which seems to imply that it had been a considerable village. Some affirm, that it took its name from Arthur king of the Britons, who was in this country about the year 550 pursuing his victories over the Danes and Norwegians. But there are no remains of antiquity at or near this place to justify such a conjecture."*

Nicolson and Burn may have been correct in their assessment of Etterby as wholly lacking *'remains of antiquity'*. The evidence from excavation has been too slender to confirm a tentative suggestion as to what kind of Roman camp – if any - may once have existed at Etterby. While it has been suggested that there might be a Roman camp at Etterby, no evidence for this has been found.

However, there is a suggestion of the Stanwix Roman fort continuing into the post-Roman period. Thus, if there is a connection with *'Arthur'*, it should be attached to Stanwix, rather than to Etterby.

The timber features at Stanwix are fairly recent discoveries. Most of the excavations there have been unpublished, so when archaeologists talk about the timber buildings these may be more examples of timber hall-like structures (such as those from the Birdoswald Roman fort). There is always a hope that the Stanwix excavations revealing the late Roman/sub-Roman timber structures will be published, but in the meantime it is interesting to know that the Carlisle Millenium Project excavation report will be available in the near future (the Carlisle Roman fort being just a stone's throw across the river from Stanwix), and very late timber structures were also found there.

FIGURE 20 - VIEW FROM THE STANWIX ROMAN FORT

The truly amazing thing about the 9.79 acre fort of Stanwix, whose Romano-British name was Uxellodunum, the *'High Fort'*, is that it is exactly between the forts of Camboglanna, where Arthur died, and Aballava on the western end of the Wall (see Chapter 7 below for my discussion of Aballava as *'Avalon'*).

This large fort also housed a force of one-thousand cavalry, the Ala Petriana, the only milliary ala (*'wing'*) in the whole of Britain. The Petriana's presence at Stanwix accounts for the name of this fort in the late 4th/early 5th century *'Notitia Dignatatum'* – Petrianis. Titus Pomponius Petra, a distinguished former commander of the unit, gave his name to the ala.

Roman historian Sheppard Frere nicely sums up the strategic importance of this fort:

> *"The western sector of the Wall was the most dangerous... both on account of the nature of the ground and because of the hostile population beyond it. It is not surprising to find, then, that at Stanwix near Carlisle was stationed the Ala Petriana... Such*

regiments are always found on the post of danger; and the prefect of this Ala was the senior officer in the whole of the wall garrison. Here, then, lay Command headquarters, and it has been shown that a signaling system existed along the road from Carlisle to York, which would enable the prefect at Stanwix to communicate with the legionary legate at York in a matter of minutes."

The fort lay on a fine natural platform today occupied by Stanwix Church and Stanwix House, a little over 8 miles from Castlesteads (Camboglanna). To the south lies the steep bank falling to the River Eden, while the land falls somewhat more gently to the north. Little is known about the fort apart from its defences. The south-west angle tower, south wall and east wall were traced in 1940, with the north wall being located in 1984. This was uncovered in the grounds of the Cumbria Park Hotel. A length of wall was subsequently left exposed for public viewing and the line of the wall marked out by setts; the exposed portion of wall lies close to the north-west corner of the fort. This and the south-west corner, a low rise in the churchyard, are the only remains visible today. Brampton Road lies more or less on the line of the south defences, with Well Lane marking the east defences. The northern end of Romanby Close lies approximately at the north-east corner of the fort.

The northern defences consisted of a stone wall with a clay rampart backing, fronted by two ditches; an interval tower was also found. The north wall was 5 ft 8 in wide with a chambered base course above the footings on the north side; the rampart backing was at least 11 ft 6 in wide. To the south of the tower lay a feature tentatively identified as an oven. The fort appears to be an addition to the Wall which was located in 1932-4 a little to the south of the north fort wall, with the north lip of its ditch found in 1984 to lie under the interval tower. A few meters further south, a turf deposit, probably a rampart, was recorded in 1997. No other trace has been discovered at Stanwix of a turf-and-timber fort, but the known fort is clearly later than the replacement of the Turf Wall in stone. The causeway over the south ditch was located beside Brampton Road in 1933. This was placed centrally in the southern defences, but this in itself gives little indication of the internal arrangements, which might have been unusual in such a large fort. Little is known of the interior buildings. A series of four parallel walls, possibly representing two barracks-blocks and lying towards the north fort wall, were examined in the school yard in 1934. A large granary was located further south in 1940.

3) THE ARCHAEOLOGICAL EVIDENCE FOR STANWIX AS ARTHUR'S POWER CENTRE

In this section I will be discussing the case that has been recently made by Ken Dark of the University of Reading for the sub-Roman (i.e. 5th-6th century CE) re-use of Hadrian's Wall, as well as of forts along the Wall and in the adjacent tribal territory of the ancient Brigantian kingdom.

According to Dark, from whose paper I will liberally quote:

> "... eight fourth-century fort sites on, or close to, the line of Hadrian's Wall have produced, albeit sometimes slight, evidence of fifth-sixth-century use. Nor is this simply a reflection of a pattern found father north; for no Roman fort site in what is now Scotland has any plausible evidence of immediately post-Roman use. Thus the situation to the north of the Wall is similar to that found in Wales.
>
> What is more surprising still is the character of the reuse found on the line of the Wall. Two sites, Housesteads and Corbridge, have evidence not only of internal occupation, but of re-fortification; at Birdoswaldthere are the well-known 'halls', while at Chesterholma Class-I inscribed stone of the late fifth or early sixth century come from the immediate vicinity of the fort. At South Shields there is also evidence of re-fortification, and there is an external inhumation cemetery. Another Class-I stone was identified by C.A.R. Radford at Castlesteads [I have rendered the inscription of this stone above in Chapter 3]. At Binchester immediately to the south of the Wall, and at Carvoran, Benwell and Housesteads on its line, there are early Anglo-Saxon burials or finds, while at Chestersand Chesterholm (perhaps sixth century)

Anglo-Saxon annular brooches come from within the forts, although these may be somewhat later in date than the other material so far mentioned.

At the western terminal of the Wall, a town-site, Carlisle, though not necessarily primarily military in the Late Roman period, has also produced substantial evidence of sub-Roman occupation, with continued use of Roman-period buildings into the fifth, if not sixth, century. Many scholars accept that Carlisle was part of the late fourth-century Wall-system, perhaps even its headquarters, and at Corbridge, the other town-site intimately connected with the Wall, fifth-and sixth century material has also been found, including, perhaps, evidence of continuing British and Anglo-Saxon use. In the North as a whole, fifth- or sixth-century evidence from what had been Late Roman towns is not common. York, Aldborough, Malton, and Catterick are our only other examples. Two of these sites (York and Malton) were part of the same Late Roman military command as Hadrian's Wall: that of the Dux Britanniarum.

It is interesting that, of the sites at Manchester and Ribchester– between the Mersey and Carlislethe only fort-sites known to have possible fifth- or sixth-century evidence – Ribchester was not only part of the command of the Dux Britanniarum, but also listed as per lineum ualli in the Notitia Dignitatum. It is, therefore, remarkable that out of the twelve fourth-century Roman military sites in northern and western Britain to have produced convincingly datable structural, artefactual, or stratigraphic evidence of fifth- or sixth-century occupation, eleven were, almost certainly, part of the Late Roman military command. Eight of these were probably within the same part of that command, and eight comprise a linear group (the only regional group) which stretches along the whole line of Hadrian's Wall from east to west. The two more substantial late fourth-century settlements adjacent to the Wall – Carlisle and Corbridge– have also produced fifth- and sixth-century evidence and two of the other towns with such evidence were also late fourth-century strategic centres under the military command of the Dux."

After setting forth these facts, and discussing them, Dr. Dark offers a rather revolutionary idea:

"Although it is difficult, therefore, to ascertain whether the military project which I have described was the work of an alliance or a north British kingdom or over-kingdom, there does seem to be reason to suppose that it may have represented a post-Roman form of the command of the Dux Britanniarum…

This archaeological pattern, however it is interpreted, is of the greatest interest not only to the study of the fifth- and sixth-century north of Britain, but to that of the end of Roman Britain and the end of the Western Roman Empire as a whole. It may provide evidence for the latest functioning military command of Roman derivation in the West, outside the areas of Eastern Imperial control, and could be testimony to the largest Insular Celtic kingdom known to us."

In another paper, Ken and S.P. Dark rebut P.J. Casey's argument for a re-interpretation of the reuse and re-fortification of the Wall and its associated forts. His conclusion for this paper reads as follows:

"If one adopts the interpretation that the Wall forts were reused in the later fifth-early sixth century for a series of sub-Roman secular elite settlements, then the associated problems involved in explaining this new evidence of occupation at that time disappear…

So, the interpretation that the Wall became a series of secular elite settlements, discontinuous from the Late Roman activity at the forts within which they were sited, is compatible with the evidence of pollen analysis, while the alternative interpretations are both rendered unlikely by it. This does not, of course, make the suggestion that this reoccupation represents the sub-Roman reconstruction of the Command of the Dux Britanniarum any more likely, but the pattern on which that interpretation is based has been strengthened, rather than weakened, by the new archaeological data, whilst the evidence also hints at a similar reoccupation with regard to the signal stations of the Yorkshire coast and their headquarters at Malton.

Perhaps, then, at last one is able to see answers to many of the most pressing questions regarding what happened in north Britain, and more specifically on Hadrian's Wall, in the fifth and sixth centuries…

The answer to all of these questions may lie in the rise and fall of a reconstructed Late Roman military command, unique in Britain, which was organized in a sub-Roman fashion reliant upon the loyal warbands of warrior aristocrats (and Anglo-Saxon mercenaries) rather than paid regular soldiers. The organizing authority of this system, probably a king of the sub-Roman Brigantes, assigned a politico-military role to the defended homesteads of these elites, and (as in the location of churches at disused forts, through land-grants?) positioned these at what had been Roman fort sites, but which were (at least substantially) deserted by the time when they were reused in this way. Thus, the 'Late Roman' Wall communities dispersed during the first half of the fifth century, but the Wall – and perhaps the north generally – was redefendedin the later fifth and early-mid sixth century on very different lines, yet not completely without regard for the Late Roman past."

I would add only that it is my belief this *'king'* of the sub-Roman Brigantes whom Dr. Dark proposes was none other than the dux bellorum Arthur.

An Arthur placed at Stanwix, with a secondary control centre at Corbridge/*'Camelot'*, makes a great deal of sense when we place these two forts in the context of the Arthurian battles as I have outlined those in Chapter 3 above. These battle site identifications (taken from the list in the HB, supplemented by the *Welsh Annals*) shows a range of conflict extending from Buxton in the south to a line just south of the Tweed, with the majority of the contests against the enemy being fought along or just off the Roman Dere Street from York northwards. The site of Arthur's death is in a fort only a few miles to the east of Stanwix and we will see in the next chapter that the location of his grave is most likely at a Roman fort just a few miles west of Stanwix.

The battle site identifications were made solely on linguistic grounds, but end up revealing a quite plausible geographical and thus strategic scenario for Arthur's military activities. When the sites are plotted on a map, the resulting pattern is compelling and, I feel, convincing.

CHAPTER 7

THE GRAVE OF ARTHUR

It is not my purpose in this chapter to deal with what I consider to be the misidentification of Glastonbury with Avalon. Others have presented a detailed case against the fraudulent claim of Glastonbury as the final resting place of King Arthur, and I added some of my own arguments in my previous book, *The Secrets of Avalon*. Here I wish to restrict my attention to the only known place in Britain to actually have born the name Avalon prior to the time of Arthur as well as to this place's proximity to both Arthur's Camlann at Castlesteads and his ruling centre of Uxellodunum at Stanwix. Obviously, the possible location of his grave at Avalon is of great interest to anyone seeking to demonstrate the reality of a historical Arthur.

Geoffrey of Monmouth's *'Insula Avallonis'* or *'Isle of Avalon'* is held by most Arthurian scholars to be a purely mythological designation - no matter where one chooses to localize it. From a philological standpoint, the –on terminal of Avallon or Avalon demands an original terminal fronted by a broad vowel. Thus there is a problem trying to equate the word with Welsh *afallen*, *'apple tree'*, or Cornish *avallen*. This problem can be overcome in two ways: 1) by evoking an attested Continental place-name, e.g. Aballone, modern Avallon, in France or by 2) allowing for the possibility that the plural form of Welsh *afal*, *afalau*, cf. Cornish *avalow* and Breton *avalou*, at some point underwent a fairly common miscopying of u/w as n.

As it happens, the only known site in all of Roman Britain to bear an *'Avalon'* name is the Aballava fort at Burgh-By-Sands, 5¾ miles west of Stanwix on Hadrian's Wall. This fort is under 14 miles west of Castlesteads. The name Aballava is found listed in the various early sources in the following forms:

- *Aballava – Rudge Cup and Amiens patera*
- *Aballavensium – RIB inscription No. 883*
- *Avalana, Avalava – Ravenna Cosmography*
- *Aballaba – Notitia Dignitatum*

It is the one spelling in the *Ravenna Cosmography* that stands out here. The v of Aballava/Avalava has been rendered as an n, yielding the spelling Avalana. This is exactly the type of spelling we would need to end up with Geoffrey of Monmouth's Latinized Avallonis.

FIGURE 21 - ST MICHAEL'S CHURCH, BURGH-BY-SANDS

The Celtic derivational suffix –*ava* of Aballava, British *-*aua*, is now found in the –*au* of Welsh, giving as a meaning for Insula Avallonis *'Island of the Apple-trees'*.

An Arthur who fell at Camlann/Camboglanna at Castlesteads could easily have been carted along the Roman road or brought down the river system in this region to Burgh-By-Sands. Camboglanna is on the Irthing, a tributary of the Eden River. The Eden empties into the Solway Firth very near Aballava/Avalana.

Two dedications to a goddess Latis were made at the Birdoswald Roman fort, 7 miles east of Castlesteads, and at Aballava. The first (RIB 1897) is addressed to *DIA LATI* and the second to *DEAE LATI*. Latis comes from a British root similar to Proto-Celtic *lati-*, '*liquid, fluid*', and Proto-Indo-European *lat-*, '*wet*'. Some authorities have seen in her a goddess of beer (cf. Old Irish *laith*, '*ale, liquor*'), but here she is manifestly a goddess of open bodies of fresh water, i.e. she is a literal '*Lady of the Lake*'. Burgh-By-Sands was, in fact, surrounded by vast marshlands. Although these lands have long since been drained, the area is still called '*Burgh Marsh*'. We can be fairly certain, then, that the Avalon fort was on an island of sorts, the '*Insula*' of Geoffrey of Monmouth's apple-tree Otherworld.

Topography dictated the position of the Aballava fort. There was an important crossing of the Solway at Burgh and the existence of this crossing may have influenced the siting of the Roman fort here. The fort sits atop a low hill on the highest ground at the east end of the village. The church sits within the south-east corner of the fort and is partly built of Roman stones. The modern road lies on the line of the Wall. Burgh is one of the least explored and understood of all the forts on the Wall. Although earlier visitors presumed a fort here, no remains were visible. Excavations north of the church in 1922, when a new burial ground was formed, resulted in the location of the east wall, 6-7 ft thick, with an earth backing, and the east gate of the fort, with a road leading out. Within the fort, stone buildings running north-south were interpreted as barracks-blocks. The Roman levels and buildings were all badly preserved.

The sketch plan of the site prepared on the basis of these discoveries suggests a fort measuring 520 ft north-south by 410 ft east-west, giving an area of nearly 5 acres. Excavations on several occasions between 1978 and 2002 south and east of the fort has led to the discovery of buildings, presumably of the civil settlement. The bath-house, south of the fort, was destroyed in making the canal, itself replaced by the railway line, now also abandoned. Further south, the tombstone of a Dacian tribesman may indicate the location of the cemetery. Recent excavations have failed to clarify the location, size and date of the Wall fort at Burgh. We do know the stone fort lay astride the Wall, but the Wall ditch was infilled and re-cut before it was constructed. It is possible that the fort to the south of the Wall at Moorhouse was retained for some time before being succeeded by a replacement astride the Wall.

As stated above, the actual Roman period cemetary at Burgh-By-Sands/Aballava is said have been to the south of the fort. When I enquired about the tombstone of the Dacian tribesman found in this cemetery, Tim Padley at the Tullie House Museum in Carlisle informed me of the discovery of two other fragments. All three are listed in the Roman Inscriptions of Britain as follows:

2046 (tombstone)

...

IVL PII... TINVS CIVES DACVS

2047 (tombstone)

D M S

...

2048 (tombstone)

VII

Alas, according to Mr. Padley, the placement of the cemetary to the 'south of the fort' puts it, in his words, 'near the vallum, possibly destroyed by the canal and railway.' The tombstone fragments were in the care of Tullie House when they disappeared.

While it is impossible to know whether Arthur was buried in the Roman period cemetary of the Aballava fort, this cemetary must remain a primary candidate for the location of his grave.

The King Who Will Be Again

In this book, I have revealed a war-leader named Arthur, of mixed North British and Dalriadan descent, who fought a dozen or so Dark Age battles before being taken to Avalon/Burgh-By-Sands to be with the Goddess of the Lake in death.

But to many – and this is as true for those who lived shortly after Arthur's time as it is for us of the modern era – Arthur does not lie in a grave at Avalon. Instead, he continues to live in a curious limbo, a place composed of equal parts continued literary and artistic invention, entertainment and gaming industry exploitation, academic specialization and Celtic/Neo-Pagan Reconstructionism.

Under the latter guise, the shift away from an Arthur who is an attestable personage has, ironically, paralleled the renewed academic insistence on the non-historicity of this northern chieftain. For while academics now, almost without exception, view Arthur as a purely legendary figure derived from folklore and developed through the medium of medieval romance, the Celtic Reconstructionists reinterpret this greatest of British heroes in a multitude of ways.

Some still hold to the age-old Messianic view that Arthur is merely being healed of his wounds by Morgan le Fay in a spiritual versus a physical Avalon. They believe that he will, in the time of Britain's most dire need (or, indeed, in the time of Mankind's most dire need), come forth to defeat some monstrous evil. Others seek to trace their bloodlines to Arthur, to his knights, to Avalon priestesses or to Grail kings in order to inherit the immense spiritual heritage that resides in the Arthurian story. There are even individuals who claim to be Arthur or, perhaps, a reincarnation of him. I have personally met a man who makes a very decent living '*channeling*' the spirit of Merlin, a spirit who with profound and pithy pronouncements advises clients on how to go about conducting their daily lives and business affairs.

This '*New Aging*' of Arthur would seem to be a harmless phenomenon, serving the positive function of bringing many new members into the Arthurian fold and contributing to a heightened level of spiritual awareness, as well as fostering a sense of '*connectedness*' with ancestors and nature in an uniquely Celtic fashion. But today's pagans need to be careful not to create alarming amounts of contrived information masquerading as inspired truth or subjective revelation that might feed naïve, inwardly-focused belief systems. These last distract us from objectively obtained realities.

As a person who himself is not immune to mystical experience, let me hasten to add that I am not advocating spiritual matters be excluded from the Arthurian orbit. Cutting off this aspect of our humanity is not only undesirable, but thoroughly impractical. The human psyche simply does not work this way. What I am pleading for is a separation of what is acknowledged as fact or reasonable conjecture from what is intuited as having religious significance. Or, to be more precise, what we choose to adhere to as tenets of belief should be based upon or extrapolated from what we know on a rational level, rather than the reverse. Be spiritual about things/concepts that actually exist or once existed. Do not give in to the temptation to readily accept as the basis for belief anything that contradicts or ignores a body of evidence assembled by decades or centuries of intense scientific effort. St. Augustine said "*I believe so that I may know*". This is a dangerous credo. Instead, "*We should know so that we can believe.*"

Furthemore, any belief system, no matter how self-satisfying, should be eschewed by anyone who truly cares about Arthur and things Arthurian if it intentionally seeks to hide potential truths from us or block us from paths that may lead to genuine understanding of deeper matters. Belief systems of this sort are usually promulgated by cult leaders who created them, i.e. those with their own often sinister agendas and need for control and profit. Any cultic use of the Arthurian tradition would be, in essence, antithetical to that tradition. Still, there always remains the danger that unusually susceptible minds could be programmed to make use of the Arthurian tradition in an unacceptable fashion. Those who wish to be latter-day Knights of *the* Round Table must guard against such a misuse of a code of conduct that, as it has been refined since the Middle Ages, promises compassionate treatment of all persons, places and things.

Most marvelous of all would be the development of a joint spiritual, aesthetic and scientific mind-set whose sole unifying purpose was to increase and enhance opportunities available for those daring individuals questing after a real Arthur. If there were a core group of people of this ilk or predisposition, the whole thrust of exploration into the possibility of an historical Arthur would not only be forever altered, but in my opinion strengthened a hundred-fold. A solitary vision forged from divergent approaches and applied with discipline and conviction to the problem of Arthur is what is required for us to be able to bring Arthur back from the Otherworld of disbelief in which current scholarly opinion has consigned him. Like the sword Excalibur, made in Avalon and rising up through the water and mist of the lake, a new paradigm in the field of Arthurian Studies must be inaugurated, implemented and sustained.

Of course, our chances of finding Arthur – of ultimately proving his historicity – depend almost entirely on finding an intact, inscribed tombstone somewhere in the vicinity of the Burgh-By-Sands fort. Natural processes such as erosion, combined with man's radical alteration of the environment and his accompanying willful destruction and occasional subsequent reuse of ancient monuments, makes the likelihood of our finding a memorial stone set up for Arthur of the 6th century an extremely doubtful proposition. Still, foolish as it may sound, it is just such an artifact that we need to be searching for. The discovery of the Cynric/Cunorix Stone at Wroxeter gives us hope that a similar stone for Arthur may someday be found at Burgh-By-Sands.

New labour saving methods of investigation now at our disposal, e.g. ground penetrating radar, allow for less costly, less invasive, less time-consuming, less bureaucratic means of finally locating and determining the nature and extent of the Burgh-By-Sand's Roman cemetery. Whole memorial stones or fragments of such stones may have been incorporated into walls or buildings. A careful visual inspection of these kinds of structures may yield significant findings. Members of the community of Burgh-By-Sands could be canvassed regarding any stones in their possession that bear what appears to be ancient writing. A correspondent who lives in the town quipped that someone could be using an inscribed stone for a door-stop! Then again, Arthur's Stone may be awaiting discovery in the foundation of the church or in the stall of a neighboring farmer's barn.

It is also vital to attempt to ascertain exactly where the missing Burgh-By-Sand tombstone fragments were found. This would entail determining who now possesses the fragments – if the parties concerned or their immediate descendents are still alive. Interviews with such people might shed important light on the cemetary's location. If private collectors of Roman artifacts can be made aware of the importance of these stones, perhaps they would be forthcoming with valuable information, especially if they were allowed to do so anonymously or were granted immunity from prosecution in the event the artifacts in question had been obtained illegally.

Archaeological excavation work is always the final resort. All too often it is undertaken in advance of a major building project as an imposed afterthought. Time, money and personnel constraints add up to produce what is all too often a hurried, haphazard and incomplete dig. Only rarely is a full-scale archaeological project proposed and executed because a site is chosen in advance for its own intrinsic merits.

I would put forward the Burgh-By-Sands Roman period cemetery as an archaeological site of astounding potential. Just imagine what it would be like to discover Arthur's memorial stone! Granted, we cannot know if a tombstone was ever made for Arthur. Nor can we know whether such a stone, if made, has survived the intervening centuries. And even if such a stone were found, nay-sayers would insist that just because a Arthur of the right period could now be placed at Burgh-By-Sands, it does not follow that such an individual was the Arthur.

However, if there is any truth to the Avalon story, and Arthur was brought to Burgh-By-Sands to be buried in sacred ground, then there is a remote chance that some trace of his presence at this fort has been preserved. And it seems to me that there must be someone out there whose destiny it is to find that trace.

Someone who wishes to prove, once and for all, that Arthur did exist.

BIBLIOGRAPHY

Alcock, Leslie. *Arthur's Britain: History and Archaeology A.D. 367-634.* 1990, Penguin, Hammondsworth.

Austen, Paul S. *Recent Excavations on Hadrian's Wall at Burgh-By-Sands* in *Transactions of the Cumberland & Westmorland Antiquarian & Archaeological Society* Vol. XCIV. 1994, Alan Sutton Publishing Ltd, Stroud

Bannerman, John. *Studies in the History of Dalriada.* 1974, Scottish Academic Press, Edinburgh and London.

Barber, John, & Elaine Lawes-Martay and Jeremy Milln. *The Linear Earthworks of Southern Scotland: Survey and Classification* in *Transactions of the Dumfriesshire and Galloway Natural History and Antiquarian Society,* Series III, LXXIII, 1999.

Bartrum, Peter C. *A Welsh Classical Dictionary: People in History and Legend up to about A.D. 1000.* 1993, The National Library of Wales.

_____. *Welsh Genealogies A.D. 300-1400* (8 vols). 1974, 1980, Cardiff.

Bidwell, Paul (ed). *Hadrian's Wall 1989-1999: A Summary of Recent Excavations and Research prepared for The Twelfth Pilgrimage of Hadrian's Wall, 14-21 August 1999.* 1999, Carlisle: Cumberland and Westmorland Antiquarian and Archaeological Society and the Society of Antiquaries of Newcastle upon Tyne.

Bieler, Ludwig (ed. & tr.). *The Patrician Texts in the Book of Armagh.* Scriptores Latini Hiberniae 10. 1979, Dublin Institute for Advanced Studies, Dublin.

Breeze, Andrew C. *Pennango Near Hawick and Welsh Angau 'Death'.* 2002, Northern History 39.

_____. *Some Celtic Place-Names of Scotland: Ptolemy's Verubium Promontorium, Bede's Urbs Giudi, Mendick, Minto, and Panlathy.* 2004, Scottish Language 23.

Breeze, David J. *J. Collingwood Bruce's Handbook to the Roman Wall.* 2006, 14th Edn. Society of Antiquries of Newcastle upon Tyne.

Bromwich, Rachel. *Trioedd Ynys Prydein: The Welsh Triads.* 1978, 2nd Edn, The University of Wales Press, Cardiff.

Bromwich, Rachel, & A.O.H. Jarman, & Brynley F. Roberts (eds.). *The Arthur of the Welsh.* 1999, The University of Wales Press, Cardiff.

Bromwich, Rachel, & R. Brinley Jones (eds.). *Asudiaethau ar yr Hengerdd*. 1978, University of Wales Press, Cardiff.

Brown, T. Craig. *The History of Selkirkshire or Chronicles of Ettrick Forest, Vol. 1*. 1886, David Douglas, Edinburgh.

Cable, James (tr.). *The Death of King Arthur*. 1975, Penguin Books.

Cameron, Kenneth. *The Place-Names of Derbyshire, Vol. 1*. 1959, Cambridge University Press, Cambirdge.

Cessford, Craig. *Post-Severan Cramond, The Heroic Age*, Issue 4 (Winter) 2001. [See Supplementary Online Bibliography]

Clarke, Basil. *Calidon and the Caledonian Forest*, in *The Bulletin of the Board of Celtic Studies*, Vol. XXIII, Part III, November 1969.

Coates, Richard. *Middle English Badde and Related Puzzles* in *North-Western European Language Evolution*, Vol. 11, February 1988.

_____, *On some Controversy surrounding Gewissae/Gewissei, Cerdic and Ceawlin* in *Nomina 13*, 1989-90.

Collingwood, R.G. *Explorations at the Roman fort of Burgh-By-Sands* in *Transactions of the Cumberland & Westmorland Antiquarian & Archaeological Society*, Vol. XXII, 1923.

Collingwood, W. G. *Arthur's Battles* in *Antiquity 3*, 1929, 292-298.

Cooper, Nicholas J. *The Archaeology of the East Midlands: An Archaeological Resource Assessment and Research Agenda*, in *Leicester Archaeology Monograph No. 13*. 2006, University of Leicester, Leicester.

Crawford, O. G. S. *Arthur and his Battles* in *Antiquity 9*, 1935, 277.

Curtis, Renee L. *The Romance of Tristan*. 1994, Oxford University Press, Oxford.

Dark, K.R. *A Sub-Roman Re-Defense of Hadrian's Wall?* in *Britannia* Vol. XXIII, 1993, 111-120.

Dark, K.R. & S.P. *New Archaeological and Palynological Evidence for a Sub-Roman Reoccupation of Hadrian's Wall*, in *Archaeologia Aeliana*, 5th Series, XXIV, 1196, 57-72.

Diehl, Ernst. *Inscriptiones Latinae Christianae Veteres* Vol. I-III. 1926-1931, Berlin.

Dyer, James. *The Penguin Guide to Prehistoric England and Wales*. 1982, Penguin Books, New York and London.

Ekwall, Eilert. *English River-Names*. 1928, Clarendon Press, Oxford.

_____. *The Concise Oxford Dictionary of English Place-Names*, 4th Edn. 1977, Clarendon Press, Oxford.

Field, P.J.C. *King Arthur's Battles, An Inaugural Lecture*, School of English & Linguistics, University of Wales, Bangor, 1995.

Foster, Idris, and Glyn Daniel. *Prehistoric and Early Wales*. 1965, Routledge and Kegan Paul, London.

Frere, Sheppard. *Britannia: A History of Roman Britain*. 1987, Routledge and Kegan Paul, London and New York.

Gover, J.E.B., A. Mawer & F.M. Stenton (eds). *The Place-Names of Wiltshire* in *Journal of the English Place-Name Society* 16. Cambridge: 1939.

Hall, J. R. Clark, & H.D. Merritt. *A Concise Anglo-Saxon Dictionary* (4th edn). 1969, Cambridge University Press, Cambridge.

Handford, S.A. (ed), & Mattingly, H.(tr). *The Agricola and the Germania*. 1971, Penguin Classics.

Haycock, Marged (ed). *Blodeugerdd Barddas o Ganu Crefyddol Cynnar*. 1994, Barddas, Swansea.

Higham, N.J. *King Arthur: Myth-Making and History*. 2002, London and New York.

Higham, N.J. & Barri Jones. *The Carvetii*. 1991, Alan Sutton Publishing Ltd., Wolfboro Falls.

Jackson, Kenneth Hurlstone. *Arthur's Battle of Breguoin* in *Antiquity 23*, 1949, 48-9.

Jackson, Kenneth Hurlstone. *Once Again Arthur's Battles* in *Modern Philology 43*, 1945-6, 45-57.

Jackson, Kenneth Hurlstone. *The Site of Mount Badon* in *Journal of Celtic Studies II*, 1953-8, 152-5.

Jarman, A.O.H. *Aneirin: Y Gododdin, Britain's Oldest Herioc Poem*. 2005, Gomer Press, Llandysul.

_____. *Llyfr Du Caerfyrddin*. 1982, University of Wales Press, Cardiff.

Jarrett, Michael G. *Non-legionary Troops In Roman Britain: Part One, The Units* in *Britannia*, Vol. XXV, 1995, 35-77.

Kennedy, W.N. *Remarks on the Ancient Barrier Called 'The Catrail', with Plans* in *Proceedings of the Society of Antiquaries of Scotland*, 1857-1860, 117-121.

Kibler, William W. & Carleton W. Carroll (tr). *Chretien De Troyes: Arthurian Romances*. 1991, Penguin Books.

Langham, Mike & Colin Wells. *Buxton: A Pictorial History*. 1993, Phillimore, Chichester.

Leach, John. *The Smith God in Roman Britain* in *Archaeologia Aeliana* Series 4 Volume 40, 1962, 171-184.

Loomis, Roger Sherman. *Arthurian Literature in the Middle Ages: A Collaborative History.* 1959, Oxford University Press, Oxford.

Mattaraso, P.M. *The Quest of the Holy Grail.* 1969, Penguin Books.

Mawr, Allen. *The Place-Names of Northumberland and Durham.* 1920, Cambridge University Press, Cambridge.

McCarthy, Mike. *Roman Carlisle & the Lands of the Solway.* 2002, Tempus Publishing Ltd., Stroud.

Mills, A.D. *A Dictionary of English Place-Names.* 1991, Oxford University Press, Oxford.

Morris, John. *Nennius: British History and The Welsh Annals.* 1980, Phillimore, London and Chichester.

_____. *The Age of Arthur: A History of the British Isles from 350-650.* 1995, Phoenix, London.

Nicolson, Joseph & Richard Burn. *History & Antiquities of the County of Westmorland and Cumberland*, Vol. 2. 1977.

Padel, O.J., & D.N. Parsons (eds). *A Commodity of Good Names: Essays in Honour of Margaret Gelling.* 2008, Shaun Tyas, Stamford.

Radford, C.A.R. *The Early Inscriptions of Dumnonia.* 1975, Cornwall Archaeological Society, Redruth.

Rivet, A.L.F., & Colin Smith. *The Place-Names of Roman Britain.* 1982, B.T. Batsford Ltd., London.

Ross, Anne. *Pagan Celtic Britain: Studies in Iconography and Tradition.* 1996, Academy Chicago Publishers, Chicago.

Rowland, Jenny. *Early Welsh Saga Poetry: a Study and Edition of the Englynion.* 1990, D. S. Brewer, Cambridge.

Thomas, Charles. *And Shall These Mute Stones Speak? Post-Roman Inscriptions in Western Britain.* 1994, University of Wales Press, Cardiff.

Tolstoy, Nikolai. *Nennius, Chapter Fifty-Six* in *Bulletin of the Board of Celtic Studies* Vol. 19, 1960-2.

Walker, J., & L. Walker & R. Sheppard, assisted by J. Brown, and K. Swainson. *Buxton, The Natural Baths: An Assessment for High Peak Borough Council*, 2nd edn. Nottingham: Trent & Peak Archaeological Trust, May 1994.

Watson, Godfrey & Goodwife Hot & Others. *Northumberland's Past as Shown in its Place Names.* 1970, Oriel Press, Newcastle-Upon-Tyne.

Watson, William J. *The History of the Celtic Place-Names of Scotland.* 1926, Edinburgh and London.

Williams, Ifor. *Canu Aneirin: Poetical Work of Aneirin.* 1938, Cardiff.

_____, *Enawau Lleoedd 40*. 1945, Liverpool.

_____ (ed). *The Poems of Taliesin*. 1968, The Dublin Institute for Advanced Studies, Dublin.

Winterbottom, Michael. *Gildas: The Ruin of Britain and Other Works*. 1978, Phillimore, London and Chichester.

Wright, R.P., & K.H. Jackson. *A Late Inscription From Wroxeter* in *The Antiquaries Journal*, Vol. XLVIII, 1968

ONLINE RESOURCES

http://www.britannia.com/history/index.html
http://www.fectio.org.uk
http://www.mun.ca/mst/heroicage/
http://www.pastscape.org.uk/
http://www.rcahms.gov.uk/
http://www.rcahmw.gov.uk/HI/ENG/Home/
http://www.roman-britain.org
http://www.ucc.ie/celt/
http://www.ucl.ac.uk/archaeology/cisp/database/
http://www.vortigernstudies.org.uk/vortigernhomepage.htm

INDEX

Long Meg and Her Daughters, 46

Lothian, 56, 68, 70, 96, 104, 113

Lugh, 68, 104

Lugus, 50, 104

Luguvalium, 50

Lune, River, 105

Lusk, 31, 32

Lyvennet Beck, 111

M

Mabinogion, 29, 103, 112

Mabon, 29, 50, 106, 116, 119

Maeswig, 107, 108

Magis, 108

Malory, Sir Thomas, 2, 15

Manapii, 32, 33

Manau Gododdin, 30, 31, 33, 37, 67, 68, 70, 71, 94, 113

Manawydan, 67, 94

Maponus, 119

Maquicoline, 30, 31, 37

Mar, 107

March, 44, 45, 46, 48

Mark, King, 43, 44, 45, 46

Marwnad Cynddylan, 97, 98

Math Son of Mathonwy, 29, 112

Matrona, 50

Medraut, 19, 21, 88, 90, 91, 92

Meirchion, 44, 45, 46, 47, 48, 49, 109

Merioneth, 44, 105

Merlin, 29, 59, 101, 134

Miathi, 71, 95

Moderatus, 91

Modron, 29, 50

Mordred, 2, 6, 14, 19, 90, 91

Moresby, 109

Morgan Fwlch, 48, 49

Morgan le Fay, 133

Moringas, 107

Mote of Mark, 6, 43, 46, 49, 50

Mothers of the Saints, 114

Mount Agned, 8, 20, 72, 76, 98, 103

Mount Breguoin, 20

Mynydd Agned, 103

Mynyddog Mwynfawr, 104

Myot Hill, 71

Myrddin. *See* Merlin

N

Nantlle, 29

National Dictionary of Wales, 110, 112

Nemetia, 79, 86, 87

Nennius, 16, 19, 24, 33, 35, 38, 40, 63, 87, 88, 94, 96, 101, 103, 113

Newsteads, 61, 62

Northumbria, 19

Nunna, 100

P

Pa Gur, 50, 67, 94, 116

Pabo Post Prydain, 104

Peblig, 112, 113

Pen Palach, 96

Peredur, 64, 65, 96

Petteril Valley, 110, 111

Petuir, 47, 48, 49

Powys, 30, 33, 34, 37, 38, 98

Pryderi, 112

Ptolemy, 32, 40, 54, 63, 89

R

Ravenna Cosmography, 89, 95, 129

W

Wear, River, 63
Welsh Annals, 87, 127, See
    Annales Cambriae
Who is the Porter?, 103
Wrmonoc, 44
Wroxeter Stone, 30, 32
Wye, River, 34, 40

Y

Yeavering Bell, 52
York, 6, 8, 64, 65, 66, 73,
    107, 111, 123, 125, 127
Ystorya Trystan, 44
Ystyuacheu, 38

LaVergne, TN USA
17 February 2011

216896LV00001B/13/P